Children of Character II

*Children of Character II
from the Early Years
to Adulthood*

Bill and Mardy Freeman

*Bill and Mardy Freeman
25467 S.W. First Avenue
Newberry, FL 32669
<u>www.thefreemans.org</u>*

CHILDREN OF CHARACTER

Children of Character II
From the Early Years to Adulthood
Published by Bill and Mardy Freeman

© 2005 by Bill and Mardy Freeman

Unless otherwise noted, all Scripture references are either direct quotations or paraphrased from the King James Bible.

Cover art by Patrick and Joel Freeman

ALL RIGHTS RESERVED
No part of this publication may be reproduced, stored in a retrieval system, or transmitted, in any form or by any means – electronic, photocopying, mechanical, recording or otherwise – without prior written permission.

ISBN: 9 781392 667332

Freeman Family Publishing
25467 S.W. First Avenue
Newberry, FL 32669
www.thefreemans.org

Fourth Edition August 2007

This book is dedicated to Jesus,
the Great Shepherd of the sheep,
who knowing us as we are,
loves us still, and calls
each of His sheep by name.

ಸಲ

*But He who enters by the door is a shepherd
of the sheep. To Him the doorkeeper opens,
and the sheep hear His voice, and He calls
His own sheep by name
and leads them out.*

John 10:2-3

Table of Contents

Foreword 9
Protecting the Weak ~ 11
Sheltering Our Children 11
Preparing the Weak ~ 29
Helping our Children Hear Our Voice 29
- Love and Accept Your Child 46
- Make Sure Your Priorities are Right 56
- Forgive your child 57
- Point them to Jesus 57
- Intercede for your child 59
- Confess 59
- Wait 60
- Ask 61
- Listen 61
- Invest in Your Marriage 62
- Commend Them 63
- Try Humor 63
- Encourage 64
- Give Them Room to Make Mistakes 67
- See Them Correctly 68
- Only Confess Your Own Sins 68
- Don't be Ensnared by Unwarranted Guilt 69
- Know When to Let Go 69
- Accept God's Answer Whatever It Is 70
- Gauge the Tension 71
- Heart Monitor 71
  - Hearts Bound Together 71
  - Hearts Growing Cold 71
  - Hearts in Danger 72
  - Hearts Broken 72

Lifting Protections as our Children Mature ~ Working Ourselves Out of a Job 85
Parental Idols and Their Consequences 89
   Lessons on Idols 92
   Idols deceive us 97
      The Idol Called Family *99*
      The Idol Called Children *100*
      The Idol Called Personal Convictions or Standards *102*
      The Idol Called Church *103*
      The Idol Called Ministry *104*
      The Idol Called a Worthy Cause *105*
      The One True God *106*
   Conclusion 118
Bringing the Weak to Maturity ~ 121
Helping Our Children to Hear the Lord's Voice 121
   James *125*
   Kate *130*
   Daniel *137*
   Hearing for themselves *138*
Giving Them the Truth of God's Grace 143
   In Regard to Laws and Grace 147
   Doctrines of Men through Interpretations of Scripture 148
   Doctrines of Men from Imitating Biblical Accounts Rather than Obeying New Testament Instruction 152
   Turning to Old Testament Standards Rather than New Testament Instruction 155
   A Few Thoughts from Bill 168
   Accepting the Unexpected 171
   Child-bearing 175
   Old and New Testament Signs of Blessing 176
   Conclusion 182
For Wives Only 183
When a Husband is Not on the Same Page... 191

Children of Character II

A Note to Dads from Bill 193
A Variation on a Theme 197
Jesus said, "Follow Me!" 203
    Our role vs. God's role 205
Acknowledgements 207
About the Authors 210
A Few More Resources from Bill and Mardy… 211
Footnotes 213

Foreword

In the secret place of most parents' hearts can be heard (if we take the time to listen) the disquieting thought that we are not the experts we thought we'd be; we all need help in this very special arena of human endeavor. Children, unlike automobiles and sewing machines, do not come with instruction books on how to take care of them.

However, if children are a gift from Yahweh-God (Psalm 127:3), then one would expect some help from Him in this regard. We are told by Solomon in Proverbs 3:6 to acknowledge our Heavenly Father as the Expert in all arenas of life, and this would include the arena of rearing children. We recognize His guidance to be essential and requisite. We also earnestly desire His guidance as that which will equip us to avoid many inadvertent yet often dreadful errors in bringing our children to adulthood. His wisdom about nurturing children is found in the Bible and is secured by a steadfast reliance upon Him to illumine our minds.

But God's wisdom on nurturing children must be grasped with the spirit and the heart as well as with the mind, and we need His Holy Spirit to energize us as parents to grasp and apply it as we relate individually to each of our children. We also benefit by real live models of what godly parenting looks like according to Biblical standards, even if their parenting is not perfect.

It is in this last respect that I have come to really appreciate the special gift that God has given to Bill and Mardy Freeman. They steadfastly acknowledge God as the Expert, and have sought to know Him as they raise their seven children. In addition, Mardy looks to the Lord in her prayer closet and tries to apply her lessons to mothering her own children. Simply put, my wife and I wish we had met Bill and Mardy and their children when our own children were still young.

In their first book, *Children of Character I*, we got a glimpse

Children of Character II

into the heart of a mom who sees each of her children as uniquely placed in her family by the Creator. Thus we found in its pages some dynamic insights on parenting that have benefited thousands since its first printing in 2001.

In *Children of Character II*, we find a mom who has struggled with the hard issues of parenting teenagers into adulthood while influencing them to be men and women of God (Acts 13:22).

It is Mardy's emphasis on reaching for the heart of young adults that has so impressed me. This approach is not only thoroughly Biblical and profoundly theological, it is also warm and genuine. The Psalmist Asaph wrote in Psalm 78:5b-8 that parents should teach the praises of Yahweh "to their children, that the generation to come might know, [even] the children [yet] to be born, [that] they may arise and tell [them] to their children, that they should put their confidence in God, and not forget the works of God, but keep His commandments, and not be like their fathers, a stubborn and rebellious generation, a generation that did not prepare its heart, and whose spirit was not faithful to God." (NASB)

The message of this book is for parents to first search their own hearts, incline their hearts to the LORD (Joshua 24:23b), and to come alongside their teens to assist them in preparing their own hearts to follow Christ. I heartily concur with its conclusions and eagerly endorse the Freemans' commitment to raising children of character, who will then be able to raise children of character, until Christ comes again – MARANATHA!

MICHAEL E. HAMPTON, THD

CHAPTER ONE:

Protecting the Weak ~ Sheltering Our Children

It is inevitable that stumbling blocks come, but woe to him through whom they come! It would be better for him if a millstone were hung around his neck and he were thrown into the sea, than that he would cause one of these little ones to stumble.
The Lord Jesus in Luke 17:1-2

Now we who are strong ought to bear the weaknesses of those without strength and not just please ourselves.
Romans 15:1

We are given many reminders in the Bible, both by example and instruction, of how imperative it is that the strong protect the weak.

Our young children are weak. They are immature and can be easily influenced or harmed. It is our job as their parents to protect them, to shelter them, while they are weak so won't be damaged by others.

One way that we protect children is by placing boundaries around them to keep harmful elements (such as dangerous people or wrong messages in what they see, read or hear) from getting to them. In this way we keep stumbling blocks at bay.

Another way we protect them is by placing restrictions (rules, laws) on them so they won't go places or see things that will cause them to stumble. In this way, we restrict them from finding stumbling blocks before they are mature enough to navigate around them. Children (the weak) stumble when they have more liberty than they are mature enough to handle.

We realize that our children will have to eventually face their share of stumbling blocks since Jesus warned us that they would be inevitable. But, we don't want to be the gate through which they come to cause our little ones to stumble. Our job is to help our children to mature and be prepared to face them by the time they come.

In this first chapter we'd like to share some of the practical ways we sheltered our children when they were young. Some things that worked for our family may not work for yours; others may. We'll also share about some things that didn't work for us in hopes that it might save others the snags we hit. We've chosen to write mostly in past tense even though we still have four children at home. It is just easier than constantly shifting back and forth between past tense for rules that no longer apply to our older children and present tense for ones that still apply to younger (weaker) ones.

We hope you are encouraged as you read.

Neighbor Children

Taking into account a verse from 1st Corinthians that says "Do not be deceived, bad company corrupts good morals"[1] Bill didn't think it was a good idea for our young children to play at neighbor children's homes if the parents didn't share our beliefs or standards. Neighbor children were welcome to play at our house, however, as long as 1) our children had finished their schoolwork and chores, 2) neighbor children respected our house rules and 3) as long as our children were not being negatively influenced.

House rules basically fell under the second commandment of the New Testament to love your neighbor as yourself. In other words: Treat others the way you want them to treat you, and if you don't want someone to treat you in a certain way, then *don't*.

Whenever neighbor children visited I asked everyone to stay within my eye contact or within earshot. I wanted to be involved in helping our children learn to play with others, as well as send a message to guests that there would be a mommy onboard at all times. When I had a warm attitude, my ever-presence was more easily received by neighbor children as well as our own children. On days when I was short with them, my presence came across as a suspicious rule-enforcer. The ideal was to try to create both a pleasant *and* safe atmosphere in which our children could play.

After a few consistently-successful visits, if I felt their play was progressing smoothly, that they had earned enough trust, I'd let them begin moving their play a little further away. How far they could play and for how long varied from child to child, guest to guest, and event to event.

Sometimes our children regressed when given new freedoms (*Mom! Miscellaneous Sibling is cheating again!*). Then we had to rein them in a little, and trust had to be re-established with several consistently-successful visits. We call this reigning-in process pulling them back in "under our wing" or "tugging on the safety leash."

> My attitude in conveying information was a key component to making it work.

People often stumble when given new freedoms, so I should have expected our children to stumble. However, I was often frustrated in those early days of parenting because my self-worth was still connected to their success (behavior), and I *needed* them to behave well.

When children came to visit, we asked our children to alert us immediately to problems with siblings or guests so we could handle them promptly. Of course, several of our children saw this as a free ticket to tattle, so we then had to address all sorts of wrong motives in the message-bearer and try to teach them how to report accurately with the right motive (let us know what was going on without jumping up and down for joy because someone else was going to be in trouble). It can be frustrating to hear that your child is getting into mischief in the next room when you just allowed him a new level of trust. It's even more frustrating when you realize you have the additional problem of dealing with wrong motives in the "obedient reporter."

The first time or two a rule was broken by a neighbor friend, I would tell him that "we don't do that in our house." I'd also give a clearly-stated warning that guests who continue doing such things would not be able to stay.

Bill asked me to please send neighbors home if a rule was broken a second or third time. I would then let them know they were welcome to return in a few days – if they kept the rules when they returned.

If neighbors continued to break the same rules when they came back, if they were disrespectful to me, if I saw that our children were being negatively influenced or were more interested in having fun than alerting me to problems, or if our children began causing problems themselves, then they would not be able to come back for a much longer period. Again, my attitude in conveying this information was a key component to making things work well.

Hand-Chosen Relationships ~ Iron Sharpens Iron

Besides trying to create a safe place in our home for our children to learn to entertain (and get along with) neighbors and guests, we also tried to encourage lasting relationships with like-minded friends. These were the beginnings of what we hoped would one day grow into iron-sharpens-iron types of friendships, where the spiritual and emotional maturity of each person was about the same, while they also shared some common interests.

We wanted our children to learn to do what was right, but we also wanted to let them have fun and memorable childhoods. To that end we tried to keep an eye out for fairly happy children who seemed to be under their parents' authority. We tried to visit with those families about once a week or sometimes every other week, alternating between our houses and theirs. We also planned times of ministry, field trips and fellowship together.

> Hand-chosen relationships have the potential of growing into life-long friendships.

Being-Discipled Relationships

As our children matured, a few more types of relationships came along. One was a *being-discipled* sort of relationship where they began to receive positive influence from people outside our family who were more mature than they were. We're not Catholic, but we liked the idea of our children having godparents. So, we asked a couple whose children were grown if they'd like to have that honor, and they've spent the last twenty-plus years happily investing in our children.

Discipling-Others Relationships

After a while *discipling-others* relationships began to bud here and there, where our children actually began to influence others for good, and then sometimes for the Lord.

We didn't let them become "teachers," though (teach

Christian materials to other children such as a Sunday school class or children's program) if we didn't think they were growing spiritually at the time. We didn't say, "Well, maybe if he takes on this important duty, he'll stretch to the material or be influenced by other teen teachers." I had taught Sunday School and Bible studies in the past and knew too well the difference between telling people what the Bible said we ought to do and actually testifying about what the Lord was helping me to do at that moment. We didn't want our children to fall into the same dangerous trap of head knowledge about God apart from heart obedience.[2] That meant that sometimes they did serve as children's teachers in Christian programs, and other times they had to pass.

Families with Different Standards

On special occasions like weddings, funerals, graduations, family reunions, etc. we knew the children would need to spend time with other children where there was a mix of standards, or a great difference in standards. Because these events weren't the norm, we tried to grant them more freedom, while at the same time give them more preparation. We let them know what they might see others do, but reminded them what we wanted *them* to do. They could play with cousins or friends out of our sight – until there was reason during that made it apparent that they couldn't.

If there was a reason, we'd pull them back "under our wing" to be with the adults for a while. This was never an exciting option for them. Alone was boring and adults just talked. Children ran, played games and had fun.

Protecting the Weak

It always helped if Bill took a few minutes to lay down the parameters of what we expected just before we walked in the door. He would either give them reminders and field questions while he was driving, or if we knew it was going to be a particularly tempting environment for the not-so-trained-yet children, he'd ask me to drive so he could sit in the passenger seat to turn around, get eye contact and make sure everyone really understood our expectations. I tried to do the same when I had the children by myself, taking a minute just before going into a grocery store or nursing home to review expectations (*Remember, we don't touch things that don't belong to us; We don't ask for candy or treats; We stay near Mom; We never wander off, etc.*). Alas, the "rules" were often comprised of *not* doing whatever happened last time. Sometimes I didn't remember to prep them and wished later I had. And sometimes my attitude was hurried or harsh and I prepped them too hastily and wounded them. Whenever I remembered to warmly invest in preparing them for a trip, they were usually responsive and the trip went much better (though not always perfect).

> Whenever I remembered to warmly invest in preparing them for a trip, they were usually responsive and the trip went much better.

My Job at Every Event:
Keeping an Eye on My Children

Whenever we spent time with others I was supposed to keep an eye and ear out for the children, whether they played near or further away. I wish I could say I did an excellent job of that, but sometimes it was easy to forget when I had the chance to chat with another mom or an in-law. Little arguments or issues would usually bring me back to my primary duty. But, not always. Sometimes, I missed problems altogether only to learn of them later.

"Say, Mom and Dad, you should have seen what Miscellaneous Sibling/Friend/Neighbor/Relative was saying/doing today!"

Sigh. Sometimes this happened a lot if a particular child wasn't responding well at home, and then it wouldn't happen for a long time which made us feel like perhaps we had "arrived." Then, it would start happening again which brought us firmly back to reality. We're constantly reminded that even the best parenting skills fall short, and only the Lord can really change a person from the inside where they don't need to be continuously monitored.

Giving in to Pressure

Overall we had a pretty good plan. We limited and monitored negative influences and tried to provide positive ones. Our children, while still immature and spiritually weak (which is what children are) were less tempted to sin, while we gained some time to help them mature.

Our plan was working pretty well until we yielded to persistent invitations from a close neighbor. I held out for a long time, but finally with Bill's hesitant okay, I gave in to pressure and let the boys start visiting. One afternoon before they left I reminded them of their responsibility to keep *our* house rules while in their friend's home. All three shook their heads vigorously in hearty agreement – before they almost knocked me over dashing out the door.

It wasn't long before I heard those famous words. "Say, Mom, guess what I heard Neighbor Friend and Little Brother

Protecting the Weak

talking about today?" It was scads more than we wanted Little Brother to know at that age, so Bill asked me to tell Neighbor Friend that the boys wouldn't be able to play for a while. I could tell that Neighbor Friend knew exactly *why* the boys couldn't play the moment I told him they couldn't. I thought one of us should tell Neighbor Friend's parents why. But, I didn't notice my husband, Mr. Non-Confrontational, picking up the phone. And I, Miss Fear-of-Being-Judged-as-Holier-Than-Thou-by-Nieghbor-Friend's-Parents, wasn't going to, either. Just the thought of explaining it to them brought images to mind of irate parents pounding on my door while Bill was at work, chanting, "Pharisees! Hypocrites!" And all the while their child throwing rocks at mine.

It wasn't surprising, then, that I began to make a connection between my desire for my children to stand alone for what was right – and my own fears of other people's opinions. It helped to remember that many of God's servants bent or buckled under peer-pressure. Here are a few examples.

- Abraham lied about his wife being his sister.
- Isaac lied about his wife being his sister.
- Jacob secretly ran away from his father-in-law's home.
- Aaron let the Israelites pressure him into making an idol.
- Aaron lied to Moses about the idol.
- Nicodemus came to Jesus by night.
- Joseph of Arimathaea became a secret disciple.
- The disciples ran when Jesus was arrested.
- Peter denied the Lord and later gave in to pressure from fellow Jews to not eat with Gentiles.

It helped to know I wasn't alone, but I still failed some of those people-pressure tests when our children were young.

Children of Character II

Here are a few lessons I learned about protecting our children while knowing we might offend someone.

1. What our children are exposed to can't be rewound or erased.
2. If in doubt about how much liberty to give a young child, it's better to err on the side of caution.[3]
3. Neighbors are important and we are to try to love them as we love ourselves. But, neighbors' opinions about how we raise our children are less important than our children's well-being.
4. Loving other people doesn't mean allowing their children to spend time with ours if our children are young or immature and we see that they will be damaged.
5. Stewardship means doing what's best for the children God has given to us *before* we try to do what's best for others or their children.
6. Just because friends are like-minded doesn't mean their children will be under their authority or bear good fruit (or even be civil).
7. We're called to love other people with God's love whether or not we agree with how they live their lives or raise their children.
8. Fear of people's opinions is energy-draining, and emotionally and spiritually crippling.[4]
9. If we're afraid we'll be judged "holier-than-thou," sometimes it's because we secretly believe we are.
10. God never allows a conflict to surface without a plan to resolve it to His glory and our good.

Protecting the Weak

A Word about Judging...

We also learned that sometimes one of *our* children was the negative influence. Those times helped me to remember that I never have the right to judge (secretly condemn) anyone or their children. We each have enough things in our own lives to keep us busy judging ourselves[5] until the end of the age.

We do have the duty, however, to judge fruit[6] (make an accurate assessment of good or bad fruit) to decide whether our children would be severely tempted, negatively influenced or even permanently damaged by spending time with someone. Being able to judge (assess) fruit without judging (condemning) is mature love, and the place the Lord wants to bring all of us.

> If we blame other people's children for influencing ours, we've missed the point. We can't blame the world for its temptations.

Taking Personal Responsibility

When we have to pull a child back in, I try to explain to friends or neighbors that it's because of things we're dealing with in our own family, not because of the influence of their child. And that is true. If our children were perfect, if we were perfect, we could both deal with any amount of negative pressure and stand strong. In reality, we have to pull our children in closer until they mature and can learn to resist temptation on their own. If we blame other people's children for influencing ours, we've missed the point. We can't blame the world for its temptations. Temptations wouldn't be a problem if they didn't find a welcoming place in us. It's our children whom we're to equip to handle temptations, and it's our children for whom we'll have to give an account. We can't blame anyone else.

Saying "No" Graciously

It helps to express this humbly to other parents if they ask why their children can't play with ours.

"I'm sorry Hugo won't be available to play for a few days (weeks, for a while, etc.). We're just feeling the need to work with him on some things right now. But, thank you so much for inviting him."

If their child truly *is* the problem (he's physically or verbally aggressive, abusive or destructive), we still wouldn't discuss it with his parents unless they asked. Unless we are very close to them, it's usually not a good idea to suggest to other parents how to raise their children as much as we think they need our help. It's far more effective to try to raise our own children in such a way that we might gain a testimony which would one day encourage others.[7]

And we wouldn't try to sneak an unasked-for opinion into our conversation.

"No, Hugo can't come over. I'm afraid he needs more work on how to handle *negative influences.*" We particularly wouldn't glance at their child when we say "negative influences" (no matter how sorely we were tempted).

Using Discernment

Even if our child is maturing at a steady clip and we feel he could handle that much negative influence, but when we pray about it and discuss it with our spouse we just don't think it would be best for him, then we still have to decline. We have to obey what we believe the Holy Spirit is directing us to do, even if others don't understand or are offended.

Keeping Our Word

When one of our sons was nine, he began playing trumpet in a Christian band program. By the time he was eleven, he'd been corrected one too many times for talking during rehearsals and not giving enough attention to the director. We didn't think he was trying to make trouble. He's naturally sanguine (more people-focused than project-focused) and was having a hard time at that age staying focused on music when people or fun were anywhere nearby.

At the same time, we knew we couldn't let him stay in an environment where he kept stumbling (disobeying the band director). We finally made the decision to pull him out of band, back under our wing, until he matured a little more.

It was hard for me to keep our word to him that we would have to take him out of band if he didn't pay attention. I knew he'd have to attend an end-of-year concert where three siblings (one of them younger) and his friends would be performing. I worried that it would be embarrassing for him. In the end I had worried too much, which is typical for many moms. It was actually less painful for him to be taken out of band than it was for me.

That experience reinforced our commitment to him that we would do what was needed to keep him inside the boundaries we'd set for him. Over the months that followed he gained time to mature, and the next year he returned to band more ready to focus.

On a side note, if a younger sibling is maturing faster, we need to avoid comparisons such as, "When you can act more like Edgar, you'll have as many privileges as Edgar." A more encouraging word would be, "Yes, Honey, Edgar does have more privileges in that area right now. You will, too, in time, I know. And do you know how pleased I am with you in so many other (fill-in-the-blank) areas?"

Technology and the Weak

High-tech communication adds a new dynamic in regard to protecting our children. The Internet, e-mail, Instant Messaging, chat rooms, cell phones and text-messaging are great communication and research tools – if used by mature people. In the hands of the immature, however, they can bring great damage.

We encourage every parent to do whatever it takes to make sure they have reliable Internet filters in place. Each of our own children's Internet browsers are cleared only for the sites they need until they become self-governing teens. We then graduate them to full Internet access with strong filters. We want them to learn to govern themselves with full access to the Internet while they are still living within our homes. That age is different for each teen. If they aren't self-governing in other areas, however, they simply aren't going to have unlimited Internet access in our home.

Internet pornography is being viewed by more teens than Christian parents realize. We've talked to a number of distressed families who found out that their sons were viewing pornography.

E-mail and Web Pages

Our children have their own e-mail accounts and web pages, partly because Bill is a network administrator and enjoys keeping his family on the cutting edge of technology. They e-mail same-gender friends. If they take online courses during high school, they also discuss course-related topics with both guys and girls on class chat boards.

Bill let them know when he opened their e-mail accounts that he retained the right to check them at any time. If a child gave us reason to check, he would. If a child gave us reason to remove it, he'd do that, too. If a child is not staying under our authority in our home, we don't allow them unlimited or confidential access to email. That isn't to say they couldn't get access to it outside our home. But, stumbling blocks are plenteous for the weak, and we don't want to be the ones through whom those stumbling blocks come.

Easily-Accessible Pornography

Children can stumble into pornography through ads in free e-mail accounts, unfiltered Internet access at a public library, or in print. A friend once told me in tears that their fourteen year-old son had started rebelling "for no apparent reason." We prayed together and when we finished I had a thought.

"Is there any possibility that your son could be accessing pornography?" I asked.

"Absolutely not," she said. "We home school and he's with us nearly 24/7. We have a good Internet filter, too."

"You're probably right," I replied. "But if he were our son and there was an unexplained distance, I would ask my husband to at least talk to him about it as a process of elimination."

My friend called a few days later. Her husband talked to their son and he told his dad that he'd been reading his grandfather's pornographic magazines for over a year. He found them in the garage on regular family visits.

If you sense a distance in your child that you just can't put your finger on, if they're shutting down for no apparent reason, don't automatically dismiss it as something that might pass.

Pray for them, and ask the Lord to help you speak to them. Get a hold of materials that will help you recognize the signs of child abuse or pornography.

Harmful People

Years ago an older couple with a children's ministry in our church asked if they could "adopt" our family. With five children under ten I couldn't have been happier. Overnight we had doting grandparents five minutes away. They came by twice a week to read books to the children, take them swimming at the YMCA or to their home to garden and play. We felt so blessed by such a giving, loving couple.

About a year or so into our friendship someone told us the man was a convicted child molester and had been violating his probation by being with our children. His wife later told us she was afraid of what he would do if she told us, so she just stayed with our children every moment they were together. This man was almost seventy years old! Our children were spared from harm by this man, but a growing number of children are violated by people that parents never suspect. Danger can come from anywhere.

Listen to this warning from a friend of ours, whose teens became involved in damaging relationships in a youth group with little adult supervision.

> "Parents should monitor activities more closely they deem "safe," like youth groups or youth activities supervised by others. One of our biggest disappointments as parents has been our own attitude that our children were finally "old enough" to be given freedom to attend programs where we trusted the supervision. We were shocked to find out that the teens

were not being supervised well at all."

Conclusion

Young children certainly are weaker. Too much freedom causes the weak to stumble, whether it's too many activities, too many toys, or too much adult-level living (the kind that requires too many self-governing decisions). That's why we who are strong are asked to bear the weaknesses of the weak. We parents, who are stronger and more mature, limit our own freedoms for the sake of our children, who are weaker and less mature. This means we limit ourselves as to where we take our children, and limit our children in their freedoms until they can eventually maneuver themselves through life with all its choices, temptations and decisions without stumbling as much as possible. The weaker a brother, the more protection (the more rules, the more law) he'll need to keep him from stumbling.

> Now we who are strong ought to bear the weaknesses of those without strength and not just please ourselves.
> Romans 15:1

We pulled the boys back from their friend's home, pulled a child out of band, and have pulled them from several other activities because they stumbled. We've also kept them from participating in some activities and from certain levels of Internet access because they were weak and prone to stumble. Protecting children when they are weak is a good thing.

CHAPTER TWO:

Preparing the Weak ~
Helping our Children Hear Our Voice

> *But solid food is for the mature, who by
> constant use have trained themselves to
> distinguish good from evil.*
> Hebrews 5:14

> *Perseverance must finish its work so that you
> may be mature and complete, not lacking
> anything.*
> James 1:4

This chapter focuses on the years that are spent helping a child make the transition from complete dependence and immaturity to self-government and maturity.

Maturity, or self-government, means that a person has developed to a place where he can govern himself (do what he ought, not just what he wants) without an earthly authority watching him to threaten or reward. He does what's right because of moral decisions he makes inside his own head and heart.

Whenever a person starts to sow seeds of faithfulness in small things (and not live just to please himself), he begins to mature. As he matures, his capacity to make more self-governing decisions increases. Our children need practice making self-governing decisions before they leave our homes. That practice begins as soon as we sense that:

- They're developing faithfulness in the home in the things we ask of them.[8] Some of us cater to our children or pamper them by asking for too little. Some discourage or anger by asking too much. If a wife circumvents her husband's firmness by asking

too little (or vice-versa), that child won't mature as quickly.
- They're beginning to making some right decisions on their own without promise of reward or pressure of consequences.
- We have their hearts – we believe they would still want to please us if we weren't watching them.

Encourage Maturity

Two very effective ways we've found to encourage maturity in our children is to 1) make sure the messages we convey to them (spoken and unspoken) are that we have confidence they will mature, and 2) reward them with appropriate liberties as they do mature. In other words, as they begin to act like adults (more self-governing, more forgiving, more mature, etc.) we begin to treat them more like adults. We gradually give them more liberties so they can continue practicing making more adult-like decisions. This is a very slow process and takes patience!

Giving Them Room to Stumble

Everyone who learns to ride a bike wobbles a bit before they find their balance. Our older children and teens need to have enough space to wobble (make mistakes and recover), and even stumble[9] while they're still under our guidance and in a safe environment. That's why we decided to let the same neighbor children come back after a few days, weeks or months – not to see if the neighbor children had changed, but to see if our children had changed – to see if they had matured enough to do what was right without a judgmental attitude. It's also why we've let some of our teens make unwise decisions, like over-committing their schedules, staying up late to finish a book even though they had a meeting the next morning, procrastinating on deadlines even though we knew they would miss the scholarship deadline or lose the internship opportunity, making a frivolous or unwise purchase, and much more. Everyone needs some experience in suffering their own consequences. Sometimes it's that hard experiences that God uses to wake us up and help us change. We still love them and let them know we'll be there to help them pick up the pieces if they make a bigger mistake.

If they don't seem to be learning from their mistakes (they're staying up late too often, showing up late to meetings, missing deadlines, continuing to over-commit, spending more money unwisely), we might tug on that line and bring them in again. We do this by first talking to them, trying to reach the heart. Secondly, depending on their age, perhaps we bring them back "under the law." That means we have to create new "rules" to govern particular behaviors. I think that might have been why Moses had to write down so many rules about behavior *(If two men are fighting, and...)* – they were probably already doing those things, and then God had to make up a new rule that said, "Don't do that anymore." New rules are always the last choice with teens. Much better to get them to comply from their own heart, mind and will, but sometimes more laws are necessary. It definitely helps to make it clear before granting new liberties that those liberties can be lost if they're misused.

The Superiority of Love

If we try to build a loving, respectful relationship during our children's early years, that bond of love stands a good chance of replacing the fear of external consequences or the hope of physical reward. But if we mistakenly measure the strength of our relationship with them by outward behavior alone, and we neglect the heart, love doesn't grow as strong and the need for controls increases. This was a crucial turning point in my parenting; I realized that my bond with the children had weakened because I sensed that if we lifted external controls, they would not do what was right from within.

Relationship between Maturity and Liberty

Few things can help an individual more than to place responsibility on him, and to let him know that you trust him.
Booker T Washington

As our children grew and matured they were gradually given more liberties. The following stages are general guidelines of how we decided when a child was ready for more liberty. [10]

> If we measure the strength of our relationship by outward behavior and neglect the heart, love doesn't grow as strong and the need for controls increases.

Little or no self-control (baby, untrained child)

- Stays mostly at home in the parent's sight.
- Supervised interaction with family members at home. Keep in mind that some sibling combinations work better than others.
- Activities limited to minimum with child-training a priority.
- When the need arises to go out, activities are limited and revolve around the proper training of the child.

Begins to demonstrate self-control at home

- Can begin short periods of unsupervised interaction with family members at home.
- Goes out more often with parents, but stays in parent's sight while out.
- Can try parent-supervised interaction with others outside the family. Keep in mind that some friends may bring out weak tendencies in your child, many times no fault of that friend.

Consistently demonstrates self-control at home

- Earns more unsupervised interaction with family members at home.
- Can try short periods of unsupervised interaction with others outside the family. Again, keep in mind that certain groups can bring out different behaviors in your child.
- Activities expand to hosting friends, helping parents host friends in the home, and playing with others in the yard or nearby.
- Child becomes more of a helper to the parent at home and outside of the home.

Begins to demonstrates self-control with others

- Child continues to earn more trust with expanded privileges and responsibilities within the home.
- Can try short periods of time being supervised by another responsible adult at home or outside the home.
- Child demonstrates self-control and discipline around others, even in difficult or trying situations.

- Activities continue to expand, especially in the area of ministry outside the home with parents or families with similar goals and values.

Consistently demonstrates self-control with others

- Continues to earn trust with expanded privileges and responsibilities within the home.
- Can try short periods of unsupervised interaction with others outside the family.
- Child consistently demonstrates self-control and discipline around others, even in difficult or trying situations.
- Activities continue to expand, especially in the area of ministry outside the home. It may even include ministry to families with differing values as you and your husband feel your child is able to have success with his behavior.

Begins to demonstrates self-control while unsupervised

- Continues to earn privileges and responsibilities based on mature behavior. Begins to act more like a mature adult.
- Earns unsupervised interaction with others outside the family for longer periods of time.
- Child consistently demonstrates self-control and discipline around others, even in difficult or trying situations while unsupervised.

Consistently demonstrates self-control while unsupervised

- The goal of our training!

- Continues to earn the right to make adult-like decisions.
- Activities expand to ministry, full-time work, full-time classes outside the home.

We've had to do our share of "winging it" and sometimes we misjudged where a child was. There was sometimes overlap, sometimes over-control, sometimes leniency, and sometimes forgetfulness or busyness on our part. And sometimes we thought it was okay to let them out further than we thought we should, or brought them in closer when we couldn't see a logical reason to. There were also times that Bill has overridden my concerns and given a child more or less freedom than I thought they should have. Even so, it worked well, and our children knew that freedoms would always be linked to maturity.

Love Your Neighbor as Yourself

We have often been asked to suggest a good curriculum for teaching character. Our experience is that the best curriculum is the example of our own lives lived out day-by-day, interaction by interaction, crisis by crisis. And the best place to start is with the second commandment – learning to love them as we love ourselves. Simply stated, that means we just try to treat them as we ourselves would want to be treated if our roles were reversed and our children were the parents, and we parents the children. We put ourselves in their shoes.

That's not to say we would treat them in a way an immature child or teen might define the second commandment, "You'd want to be left alone if you were me, so just leave me alone and let me do what I want!" No, we would try to love them in the way we know we would want to have been loved by our parents when we were teens – with safe boundaries and respect, kindness and sincerity, and not with either leniency and license or strict rules and strong expectations. We are old enough and wise enough now to see that simply getting away with sin isn't love; it's neglect. We also understand that over-correction and harshness would only have driven us further away from our own parents.

Trying to learn how to love my children as myself I begin to think, "How would I have wanted to hear correction if I had just been caught doing that? What would love look like to me if I realized I had just broken my own parents' hearts?" God has given us sound judgment and a working conscience to understand and answer those questions. Being encouraged when I made a good decision would have also helped me when I was growing up, so I understand that encouragement will help my children, too.

Unless our judgment is terribly clouded by other issues, the answers are usually obvious. But, our judgment *is* often clouded by other issues!

> Now may the God of peace…equip you with all that is good to do His will, working in us what is pleasing in His sight, through Jesus Christ, to whom be glory forever and ever.
>
> Heb 13:20-21

Pursuing God Rather than Good Fruit

In my early days of parenting, I didn't realize I was relating to my children through my own needs for validation, approval and acceptance rather than genuine love. I saw that bearing fruit for God was important; it was a sign that we loved God. I wanted to love God, so I wanted to bear fruit for Him. As a

Preparing the Weak

young mother "good fruit" meant raising godly children. Godly children, therefore, became very important. Because of this, my self-worth was woven pretty tightly into my role as a parent, so that success (my children's attitudes, behaviors and choices) was very important to me.

We work hard for what is important to us and I was diligent in my parenting. The only flaw in my plan was that it wasn't working. I wasn't producing very good fruit. My bad fruit forced me to reevaluate my "gardening methods."

What I discovered was that I'd been pursuing fruit more than pursuing God. This invisible misplaced focus disguised itself as love, but caused all sorts of problems. Our daughter, Kate, remembers life in those days.

> KATE: I was in trouble a lot in those days, and I remember by the age of eight feeling inside that no matter what I did, and no matter how well I did it, it would never be good enough. I felt like giving up trying to please my parents.

I had no idea our daughter was feeling like that at the time. I was a busy mother of many young children. From my perspective, I may have had a splinter in my eye in being a little too harsh in some of my responses to her, but she had a log in hers in that she kept doing things we asked her not to. And the more I corrected her, the more she misbehaved. I could see that she was in need of correction more frequently, but that only served to frustrate my busy self even more.

It was my own wrong reactions to my children's need for correction that God kept using to open my eyes to my own need for change. Instead of genuine concern, there was still some anger, frustration, disapproval, judgment, coldness or panic, depending on the day, circumstance, offense or the child. I was beginning to see that these responses were rooted in fear (that my children might rebel) and pride (which would be dashed if they did).

Call to the Lord

When I saw I needed more change in order to reach Kate, I felt pretty discouraged. So discouraged, in fact that I felt like I would never be able to change. That can be a very bad place to be, if we think, "I'll never get this right. I keep making mistakes and my heart doesn't change. I might as well give up." But, it can be the very best place to be if we turn to God and say, "I'll never get this right! I keep making mistakes. Lord! Will You please, please help? You may do whatever You wish to fix my *own* heart."

I think of this kind of prayer like a call to a service repairman. When our dishwasher broke and the problem was beyond Bill's expertise, he asked me to call a repairman. It was the first time in our marriage I had ever called for repair because he or one of the boys had always fixed everything. It felt

> The Lord is near to all who call upon Him, to all who call upon Him in truth.
>
> Ps 145:18

novel to pick up the phone and ask someone else to come into our house to fix something we couldn't. Do you know what happened after I called? The repairman came! Just like he said he would! Even though he'd been (theoretically) driving past my house every day for years, once I'd actually made the call, actually authorized him to have access to my dishwasher, he came. In addition, he knew exactly what was wrong and what needed to be done. Bill didn't know. But the repairman did. And the reason he knew? It was his job to know. I couldn't understand the problem, and Bill couldn't fix it for me. I had to authorize (grant permission) to the one who knew how to fix it. Oh, how happy I was to have a working dishwasher again.

This analogy is very real for me. As long as it's my responsibility to "fix" my own heart, I feel as helpless as if I were staring at the wires hanging out of my broken dishwasher. How do I even know where to start? I feel as though I might as well not even try. But as soon as I realize that all I have to do is call and ask the One who knows how to fix it to please come and figure out that mess for me, that He would actually come if I called (authorized Him to), that it was His job to do the work, and that I didn't have to understand what He was doing, that I only had to "open the door,"[11] well, happy day! Prayer is simply asking God for help.

Some of my most effective prayers have been just like that S.O.S. call to the dishwasher repairman. I don't have to try to figure out the problem, wait until I can understand it, fix it myself, or even feel like saying a spiritual-sounding prayer. I can just ask my Heavenly Father with a word to dispatch His skillful Holy Spirit to get to work on the problem. Many times I've prayed, "Help, Lord! I know my heart is a mess! I don't even feel like praying about this. But I give You permission to work on my heart, to do whatever it takes to change it. You have my invitation and my okay to remove anything that doesn't glorify You." Sometimes I sense an immediate lifting of my problem. Sometimes I don't feel any better, but then I notice over time that my heart begins to soften a little, or I begin to discern a little better. Or my negative feelings don't automatically peg-out to 10 on the Momzilla-scale, but instead drop to a 3, 5 or 7.

One thing we don't want to do is *purpose* to love others with God's love. Purposing to do God's will is simply another way of saying we're going to accomplish God's will as an act of our own will, or that we can *will* ourselves to do God's will. If we take any instruction from the Bible – "be holy in all your behavior" from 1 Peter 1, for example – and say, "Lord, I purpose to be holy in all my behavior," but we isolate that verse from the rest of the New Testament that clearly explains the "how-to" that it is *Christ working in us*, helping us to do His will, we will fail. The good news is that God is both willing and able to help us do His will. I have found it much more effective to *purpose to call on the Lord for grace, mercy and help* each day.

The Lord seems to be committed to ferreting out all the little passions and desires that we let slip into His place in our hearts. For us moms, they're often revealed through our children. When He brings those issues to light, our part is to call on Him and obey His voice. His voice will never tell us to do what we can't ("Fix your own heart, My child."), but what we can ("Confess your fault, My child."). His part is to do the fixing in our hearts that makes us able to confess. Without these continual changes in my own heart, I would never have been able to come to enough maturity to help guide my children to maturity.

I placed that call to the Lord to begin working on my heart in my responses to Kate. Unknown to me, she noticed the difference right away.

> KATE: I knew I was causing trouble around the house, and I knew I was wrong. But what struck me was that for the first time I didn't have to change first to receive my mom's love and approval. The verse, "We love Him because He first loved us" became very real to me at that time because I felt like I was experiencing it. I didn't make any changes in myself, but I was suddenly the recipient of my parents' unconditional love. That made

me want to love them. It made me want to please them. I began to love them back because they first loved me.

Relating to a Child Based on His Needs

If we relate to our children based on our own parental needs (those invisible, hard-to-detect needs based on selfishness, fears, pride, guilt, etc.), our children will feel that negative pressure, no matter what else we say or do to counteract it. This is true even if we don't realize we're doing it.

We want to relate to our child based on *his* need. That is love! Love says, "It's good for you to have some safer boundaries so you can mature a little more, but even if you fail and must face the consequences, I still love you." We give them affirmation and affection because they need it, not because it makes us feel warm to give it. And we give firm boundaries and consequences because they need them, not because we need to have them not interrupt us, need them to validate our reputation, fulfill our dreams for them or turn out a certain way.

> Bonds based on the parent's needs are negative and unhealthy.

This is the same way our Heavenly Father deals with us, commanding that we worship Him, not because He is needy and must have worship, but because He knows we need to worship Him. He loves us and wants what is best for us, and He knows worshiping Him is good for us.

When one of our adult children asked how I would feel if he wanted to have a very private, family-only wedding, my immediate answer was, "Honey, your wedding will belong to you and your bride. We'll help you in any way we can to make it what you want it to be." Later I realized I was saddened by the thought of a private wedding. I felt like something I'd been looking forward to had been lost. I took a quick look at the second commandment, to love my neighbor as myself, and realized that I was sad because *I* would miss out on having *my* friends and *my* relatives rejoice with *me* over the marriage of *my* child. I had to laugh at my perspective because I could have told any other parent that a wedding isn't about parents, but the bride and groom. We're not supposed to give it to them with strings attached *(I want to make your gown, bake the cake, plan the reception, invite Uncle Freddy[12])*. I suddenly felt grateful for the freedom Bill and I had to plan our own wedding without parental expectations. How practical God's Word is! If only I would place myself in other people's shoes more often and love them like I want to be loved.

Bonds that are based on a parent's needs are negative and unhealthy. They say, even without words, "I need you to behave in a certain way. Don't you see how you're hurting (disappointing, killing, etc.) me (your father, our family, God)? Why must you always…? Why can't you ever….? When are you ever going to start….? When are you ever going to stop…?" Those types of negative statements are clues that the parent is seeing their child as someone who should meet their needs, and their child is disappointing them. It creates a no-win environment for that child, for no person can fulfill the unmet emotional needs of another.

It is much easier on a younger child to suffer physical consequences such as being on restriction, losing a privilege or getting a spanking (that isn't in anger), than to suffer the emotional consequences of cool emotions, demeaning words or cruel anger from a parent. Their hearts can begin to harden by their time they're in their teens, which leads them to rebel against more restrictions.

It was another three years, around age eleven, before Kate

surrendered her heart more completely to the Lord and then gave her heart back to us. Little by little, issue by issue, God was multi-tasking, working in my heart first, and then hers, revealing to both of us our need for Him.

Remember that Teens Have Strong Emotions

Do you remember when you were a teen, how strong your emotions were, how quick your judgments? I was born again as a teen and experienced an indescribable lightness and joy for weeks, my motivation being to please the Lord in everything I did. One day I was in the home of a Christian friend when a man stopped by to see her. I greeted him, but he was aloof toward me and only spoke privately to my friend. After he left, my friend told me he was her pastor, and that he told her I couldn't have really been born again because a Christian wouldn't dress as I did. It was the 70's and I was dressed like I always was on a hot summer day – in jean shorts and tee-shirt. I was devastated. My parents weren't Christians at that time and their own issues took all their attention. I received very little guidance of any kind.

That experience, over thirty years ago, has helped me in several ways. I remember how strong feelings are in the teen years, and how easily someone's words can devastate or inspire. I also remember what it feels like to a teen to be judged by an adult who sees himself as closer to God than others.

Love Yourself

Jesus said the second greatest commandment was to "love our neighbor as we love ourselves."[13] Doesn't it sound selfish to say that we love ourselves?

Children of Character II

Coming from a dysfunctional childhood with alcoholism, drug abuse, tragedy and neglect, I understand how intangible this concept of loving one's self can seem. When you have received very little positive attention or worthy investment for your first eighteen years of life, you can feel invisible, unworthy, non-valuable and non-person-like. The subconscious message is that you weren't valuable enough to invest in in the first place. This feeling causes us to look outside ourselves for things more worthy of investment (other people, great causes, even God).

Yet, a child raised in an overbearing, over-investing or perfectionist home can feel the same way, just for opposite reasons *(No matter how much they invest in me, I never seem to be able to be good enough/reach their standard. I'd better look outside myself for something more worthy to pour my life into.)* It's easy to see how impossible it would be for us to "fix" ourselves. We wouldn't know how to begin.

> We don't serve God to gain His acceptance; we are accepted so we serve God. We don't follow Him in order to be loved; we are loved so we follow Him.
>
> Neil Anderson

But, tucked tightly between the first command to love God and the second command to love others, something begins to happen. When we turn to God to try to love Him, we see that He has already poured His love on us first. Before we were saved, before we've dealt with all those how-we-dress matters, or need-for-control tendencies, before we've made things right with others, He just loves us. Exactly as we are. Before we've changed, and even if we don't change. God loves us exactly as we are, even in our worst moments.

Take a moment to think about what you believe is your worst sin – the darkest side of you that perhaps no one else knows about. Do you sense that God loves you in spite of that sin? It still causes you shame, but do you know that you know that you know that God sees it and loves you just the same? That is the truth – He is love and His love for us never changes. We will grieve His Spirit, we will break His heart, but His love for us is unchanging and forever.

To love ourselves as God intended, we have to believe that His love reaches that far.[14] That's when we begin to get a picture of how much we are truly loved. When we can accept that love (we'll never understand it), we begin the journey of loving ourselves the way Jesus meant. Once we begin to love ourselves in that way, loving our children in the same healthy way gets much easier.

Each time we have to face something unpleasant, we find out a little more about our true selves. A teen that disappoints us can be an unpleasant experience. It may stir up unresolved memories from our own teen years, which stirs up fears or guilt that add more negative emotion to our relationship. But with each inch of God's love for us that we yield to in the darkest parts of our hearts, a tiny new ray of lightness appears inside. Understanding begins to replace anger, forgiving ourselves replaces self-condemnation, love displaces fear. We're then a little more able to look past our child's actions to his heart. We remember when we also did or said things that were hurtful, damaging or selfish. We begin to be as understanding and forgiving with others as we're learning to be with ourselves.

> Once we begin to love ourselves in that way, loving our children in the same healthy way gets much easier.

The more I allow God's love to penetrate the hard pockets of my heart that are revealed through bumping up against crises in daily living, the more I'm able to accept (and love) myself. Without His love entering first, though, my love of self is skewed like the world's preoccupation with self-love: *Me first!* But with God's love? It's a perfect love, one that says, "*My* anger is out of control, Lord. Help *me* to be changed into Your image," or, "*My* spirit is willing, but *my* flesh is weak," so instead of condemning myself for that fact, I can say, "Dear God, please help *me* to guard *my* heart," or, "*I'm* so drawn to the world lately, Lord. Will you help *me* to know how to renew *my* mind so I can know You better?"

When that kind of self-acceptance begins to appear, it brings with it a connection with the rest of the human race and a new compassion for others, so we can truly begin to love our neighbor as ourselves. And our closest neighbors are only a room away.

Love and Accept Your Child

The beginning of love is acceptance. It's the foundation on which the rest of a relationship is built. Love doesn't say, "I'll love you if…", or, "I'll love you when…." Love accepts the one loved as they are and where they are, whether they ever change or not. *For God so loved the (unchanged, unrepentant, undeserving) world…*

That doesn't mean we don't want others to change. Wanting someone else to change can be rooted in wanting what's good for them. God wants all men to be saved and come to the knowledge of the truth. That's love. *Needing* someone to change is based on what we think is good for us. That's selfishness, not love. God doesn't *need* us to love Him. Need can disguise itself as love, but it will expose itself if the object of our "love" doesn't do the things we need. Deep down inside, we should know whether we *want* or *need* our child to change.

It helps to imagine for a moment our worst-case scenario, and then take a look at what bubbles up from the bottom of our heart. Sorrow, understanding and compassion for our child? That's love. Fear, panic, frustration, indignation, anger? Those are probably signs of misplaced parental needs.

Accepting a child as he is was hard for me to accept. How could I accept him exactly where he was? Did it mean I had to accept his disobedience? His disrespect? His rebellion? It seemed risky as though I was being asked to tolerate sin in him.

Accepting our children exactly where they are doesn't mean we approve of where they are or agree with what they're doing. It means we accept the fact that they're where they are – and we love them anyway. Denying or ignoring the fact that they are where they are won't make their problems go away. Not facing the truth of where our child really is will not make him change.

Our son, James, was a compliant and happy child, but he struggled with academics. Memorizing phonics and math drills in his early years brought him to tears, and caused me to vacillate between feeling like an ogre and a failure as we plodded on.

When things didn't improve in his early teens, and his attitude began to slide, I panicked. I began putting more pressure on him to work harder, better, longer. But I could tell I was going to lose the heart of this easy-going, beautiful young man if I kept the pressure on.

I finally began crying out to the Lord for help. When I did, I realized I had been trying to cram him into an academic mold he wasn't cut out for. The Lord helped me to come to a place of being able to accept James exactly as he was, with all of his gifts and talents and warm, loving nature, along with his level of learning. Once I accepted him, I felt more comfortable adjusting his curriculum to his bent and his calling. His natural talents then began to blossom even more.

James is 21 at this printing, and writes about the shift he felt in being accepted and loved for himself.

JAMES: When I was in my early teens I fell more and more behind in some of my schooling. Math, grammar and spelling were always hard for me. But I did very well in the things I enjoyed. I loved working on things and fixing things. I also liked music and loved reading. But still, I was falling behind in other areas. It wasn't that I didn't want to do the work. In fact, I wanted to please my parents very much. I just couldn't understand most of the concepts.

There were several things my parents began to do that helped me get through those years. They let me start learning at my own pace, and they allowed me to work on things I enjoyed. They also kept telling me how much they loved me and began praising me for the things I did well.

Being allowed to start succeeding in the things I could do well was very encouraging to me. Not being scolded for the things that I couldn't do helped me as well. If I'd been told I was just stupid or that I couldn't do things other children my age could do, that would have made it harder for me to catch up later on.

I already knew by the time I was twelve or thirteen that I wanted to be a landlord. I wanted to provide clean, affordable homes for families to live in. My parents allowed me to work on certain projects around the house and let me spend a few weeks with another family that was also going into real estate. That was like ice cream for me through the harder years of school.

It really helped me through the last four or five years of school to know what I wanted to do, and to be able to work toward that goal as a part of my school.

Preparing the Weak

Because I no longer needed James to fulfill my image of who I thought he should be (someone who could master certain levels of academics at a certain age), we were able to design a two-year school plan for him that included reading classics and other inspirational works (which he loved), working and traveling with his dad (which he enjoyed), learning some computer work (which he liked) and working on fix-up projects around the house (which he really loved and excelled in). He later returned to math, grammar and spelling and found they had become much easier with time. At this printing, James is well on his way to becoming a successful businessman, having bypassed traditional college and instead graduating from a four-year trade school while working full time. He recently purchased his first condo without going into debt, and happily spends every free moment after work fixing it up to resell and start over.

> Behold, I make you fishers of men.
>
> Matthew 4:19

Seeing and accepting a child where he really is can be stressful. Stress has been defined as the distance between expectations (or need) and reality. The greater the gap, the greater the stress. It usually hurts. It unearths all those needs in our hearts that God wants to meet Himself. If we confess those needs as we become aware of them, we'll find Him faithful to begin filling or replacing them. We just have to be sure to place that Heavenly call to the Great Physician so He can start cutting away the things in our life that keep us from accepting our child.

Jesus compared evangelism to fishing, the idea being that we're to be bringing in men's hearts for God. A hook-and-line fisherman of today knows he needs just the right amount of tension on the line between him and his catch. This is a good picture of the invisible line between our children's hearts and us. If there's too much tension (strong expectations, more emphasis on standards than the relationship, strong parental needs, legalism or strict external controls), the fish will either be too afraid to ever learn to swim on his own, or will try to swim away. On the other hand, too little tension (leniency, license or neglect), and the hook is never properly set and the fish wanders. With some gentle tension, we can help draw them in closer to us and hopefully closer to the Lord.

We might compare great parenting to emulating a great football coach. If the players sense their coach's motives are right and that he cares about them, they'll try to please him. They'll give more than they normally would, more than they ever thought they could, because they sense he's dedicated to them and their team's success. Paul reminds me of a dedicated coach when he writes to the Thessalonians, "You are witnesses, and so is God, how devoutly and uprightly and blamelessly we behaved toward you believers, just as you know how we were <u>exhorting</u> and <u>encouraging</u> and <u>imploring</u> each one of you as a father would his own children, so that you would walk in a manner worthy of the God who calls you into His own kingdom and glory."[15]

A coach (or a parent) who's in it for any sort of personal gain, or who finds himself a coach when he didn't expect to be, or who is concerned about his own glory will have trouble winning the hearts of the players. They just won't be motivated to please him once they sense his true motives. A very mature player might continue to push himself for the good of the team, but he'd be demonstrating more wisdom and maturity than his coach.

If our children are very obedient when they're younger, we may believe that our bond between them is strong. All looks well. But it's the bond of love (not just outward obedience) we want to strengthen while they're young. Love is the path that instruction will need to travel on later.

Preparing the Weak

When Kate was sixteen, we let her sign up for an online coed class where, unknown to us, e-mail correspondence about class topics continued after the course ended. At the same time she had replied to some e-mails from some young men, Christian friends she'd met while working in Christian events in other cities. This was new territory for our family, so she didn't know that we wouldn't approve.

Decisions about what is best in areas like this are different for each family and sometimes for each child. Bill told Kate that for our home, coed correspondence during class about class was fine, but he felt that online correspondence with young men about non-class topics should wait for a couple of years. Kate didn't agree with her dad. She had a number of friends whose e-mail wasn't restricted in this way, and she was disappointed. But she assured us she would comply.

In the mean time I felt a new distance between us, and noticed that it produced a worry, a stress in me that I hadn't experienced in a long time. I had to let go of my expectations of what I felt that her response should be, so I could still respond to her in love.

When we have to pull our child away from negative or unprofitable places or people, it feels like we're pulling them away from the edge of a cliff. We can see the danger. Everything in us is on the alert that they might fall and crash. That awareness can cause us to pressure them to come away from the cliff, to try to hold onto them with pleadings, lectures, advice or threats.

That is where God can come in for both parent and child. He wants us to "let go of them," – not throw our hands in the air and give up on them, but let go of our own *need* for them to be safe. This helps them to be freer to possibly hear the Lord's voice in their hearts without our voice in their ears drowning it out.

Over the next few days I noticed Kate was quieter than usual.

When I asked her how she was, she'd say, "Fine." When I finally asked her if we could talk about it, she said she felt she'd worked hard to earn our trust, and wanted to continue to be trusted in this new area of e-mailing Christian young men. The more I tried to explain to her what could happen, the more she camped on the trust issue.

One morning I remembered a sort of Bambi-needs-his-mother's-protection story that we'd read when she was little. I tapped on her door for a teasing-but-still-to-the-point sort of chat.

"Say, do you remember that story about how that baby deer needed its smart and caring mother's protection in the big, bad forest?" I batted my eyes when I said "smart and caring."

Kate picked up on it immediately and said, "Yes. But what if the mother deer was overreacting and trying to protect the baby deer when the baby deer was mature enough to go to a safe place in the forest?"

"Oh, that story was not about the mother deer, but the baby deer. She might not recognize the dangers that the mother deer knows are there."

"But shouldn't a mother deer trust God with her baby deer? Perhaps the mother deer is in need of more faith."

I could tell it was going to be a long conversation. She continued.

"And if the baby deer has been trustworthy thus far, shouldn't she be trusted that she will come right back if she sees danger?"

"But the mother deer wouldn't be a good mother deer if she let her baby deer go places that are unknown and potentially dangerous."

"But, the baby deer *isn't* going to go to any place that's dangerous. The baby deer wishes the mommy deer trusted her on this."

"Oh, the mother deer *does* trust the baby deer very much. But there are certain places, certain *fields*, the mother deer wouldn't want her baby deer to play even though she trusted her."

She paused. "So it's the 'field' the mother deer doesn't trust?"

"Of course. What do you think the baby deer might have thought it was?"

"Well, the baby deer *might* have thought that the mother deer thought there was *something in the baby deer* that couldn't be trusted."

Not until that weird third-person deer-chat did I understand that my daughter was hurt because she thought we saw something lacking in *her*, and that we didn't trust *her* to navigate her way through conversations with one nice Christian friend and several classmates. She also thought we saw a danger in those specific friendships that she couldn't see. When she realized it was the *field* of coed correspondence where we didn't want any of our younger teens to go, she understood. I had managed to let go of my need for Kate to be safe, and that made it much easier for me to reconnect with her and reestablish our bond. She stopped "pulling on the line," responded to the Lord, and the distance between us evaporated.

When another one of our children was becoming more rebellious around the age of ten, I wanted some kind of assurance from God that if I did pop that release inside and let go, that He would catch him and keep him from falling – spiritually, morally and physically. Finally, after much internal wrestling, I settled that it would be enough if He would just save his soul.[16] As I poured out my heart to the Lord and He began to reveal all the needs in me that kept me from letting go, His gentle Spirit put a tiny thought into my head.

Children of Character II

And if he crashes and dies, or if he rejects the Lord, will You love and follow Me still?

That question was a crucial turning point in my parenting: I had to choose my God that day – my child or my Heavenly Father. Until that hour, I hadn't even realized there was a conflict between the two.[17] They had seemed meshed as one and the same: if I loved God I would do everything in my power to keep my child from falling.

There were no Heavenly guarantees for me that day, only a gentle nudging to obey the Lord and pop the release – to let go, no matter the personal cost.

We might have the parental tools to "reel a teen in" from the edge with external restrictions, consequences and rules, but without bonds of love we won't be able to keep them with us long enough to get them ready for the next cliff or the next. And if we try to jerk them in, the line might break. That doesn't mean we lift the external rules and consequences - Kate still couldn't e-mail young men and sometimes our boys had to pull weeds when their attitudes were bad. It means we "pop the release" inside of us, and let that child completely go – to God.

If there is a lot of damage that's already occurred between you and your child, take heart. Many parents in our generation

> And again I say to you, it is easier for a camel to go through the eye of a needle than for a rich man to enter the kingdom of God." When His disciples heard it, they were greatly astonished, saying, "Who then can be saved?" But Jesus looked at them and said to them, "With men this is impossible, but with God all things are possible.
>
> Matthew 19:24

Preparing the Weak

weren't won to Christ or discipled to maturity by their parents. God found us *despite* our backgrounds. He can do the same for our children. Has your teen moved out against your wishes? Is he seeing someone he shouldn't? Is he in an immoral relationship? Has she gotten pregnant, had an abortion, or married without your blessing? Perhaps your son has broken the law, used or sold drugs, spent time in prison, or told you he's rejected your faith? There is hope! As a matter of fact, there is *more* hope for them than for a moral wealthy person! Jesus said it was His mission to call *sinners* to repentance, but that it is easier for a camel to go through the eye of a needle than for a rich man to enter the Kingdom of Heaven. *All things* are possible with God!

> God is very good at multi-tasking, working on everyone's hearts in a conflict. We can expedite His work in everyone's heart if we get busy yielding ours.

God will often use those outside the family in bringing a wayward teen or adult child to Himself. But, if you'd like to be a key player in winning your child back to Jesus, there are many things you can do. First and foremost, cry out to the Lord *for yourself* every day. I try to do this by praying the Lord's Prayer with sincerity. It seems like a self-focused prayer (give *us*, forgive *us*, lead *us* not into temptation, deliver *us* from evil…), and it is! We're to guard *our own hearts* with all diligence! Jesus told His disciples several times to pray for themselves. He also intended for us to pray the Lord's Prayer every day, because it says, "Give us this day (not this week) our daily bread."

After praying that prayer, give God permission to do anything He wants to in your own heart through this trial of raising your child *(Your Kingdom come – in my heart, Your will be done – in this situation)*. Sometimes that dishwasher repairman will linger a few moments and explain exactly what he found. Other times he'll just fix it and go. Ask the Lord to show you anything He thinks you need to know and ask Him to heal the rest. Be sure to obey anything He brings to mind – a fault that needs to be confessed, a sin that needs to be forgiven, or a sense that you should be praying a certain verse for you or your child. Make sure you are getting – and keeping – a clean conscience.

Make Sure Your Priorities are Right

Our chief objective in every trial is to be conformed to the image of Jesus.[18] If we sense our objective is to straighten out our child, we'll probably lose him. If we have hidden motives of making personal changes for the purpose of winning our child back, and not for the purpose of really submitting to our Heavenly Father, those motives will be exposed, too. And our child will feel manipulated and probably pull away even more.

It can't be a partial surrender to God. Of course, we'll discover as we go along that we have many more things to surrender. The work in our hearts is never complete after the first altar. But God is very good at multi-tasking, working on everyone's hearts in a conflict. We can expedite His work in everyone's heart if we get busy yielding ours.

Our spirit and attitudes are easily discerned by our family. They speak volumes about us, and reveal where our priorities lie – influencing the people we love for either good or bad.

If our motivation is changed from wanting to fix our children to wanting to please our God, then our children can still make wrong choices and even fail while we grow stronger and become more peaceful. This serves as an incredible witness to them. And they need all the examples of true Christianity they can get!

Forgive your child

Forgiveness is clearing the path between us and another person. There might be stumbling blocks of offense we've dropped there, or they've tossed there, or both. Offenses make navigation back and forth along the path to each other very difficult. Forgiveness is not waiting for them to remove the blocks they put on the path; it's walking up to their offense, picking it up, carrying it over to the Savior and leaving it there. It's removing it for them. The more offenses we remove through forgiveness, the easier it will be for them to navigate their way down that path back to us.

We have to forgive our children of everything they've done against us, and the quicker, the better. We also have to forgive them of anything they've done against themselves. It's terribly painful to watch a child make damaging choices or destroy himself, but if we hold on to unforgiveness, we actually add to the damage and hinder our own spiritual freedom as well.

Point them to Jesus

Helping your child see the way to Jesus isn't easy. Listen to the testimony of our son, Daniel.

DANIEL: Before I started my quiet time, my parents seemed to be my conscience and if I got away with something, it really didn't bother me too much. When my parents asked me to start having my own "quiet time," my conscience started bothering me. That's because it started working better. It bothered me so much it was hard to concentrate on school and other activities because I was thinking about a sin I'd been doing.

I'd wanted to tell my parents about my sin and get my conscience clear, but I was afraid. It was like a circle of deception that kept on going around and around, and seemed impossible to get out of. My parents sensed I had something on my mind.

My mom would ask me if there was anything I needed to tell them. Most of the time I would say, "No," and then I would add that lie to my list of things that were bothering me. My prayer life and Bible time were also falling apart because I didn't want to be alone with God. I also didn't want to be alone with my dad, either. I was afraid I'd have to confess my sin to him.

I soon became afraid of the dark and of being alone because I didn't think I could trust in God to protect me. I thought He'd want to punish me for hiding my sins. I wanted to do great things for Him, but I couldn't get past my sin.

One night my mom explained to me that there are three parts to my life:[19] my public life, my personal life and my private life.

My public life looked pretty good – it was when I was outside my home and with other people.

My personal life was how I acted around my family, how my school was going, and my attitude toward my parents and siblings. That wasn't so good. My school took a long time to get done. I didn't have a very good relationship with some of my brothers, and I always acted like I was trying to evade my parents (because I was).

My private life was what I did when no one else was watching, including my prayer and Bible time. No one knew about my private life except God and me. I knew it wasn't in order.

It really helped when my mom started coming to my

room and checking with me at night, right before I went to bed. She told me she loved me, and asked if there was anything I needed to talk about with her or my dad. Then she would pray with us.

Finally one day my parents caught me in my sin, and I ended up confessing all those things that haunted me. I was glad to get them off my chest, and it was most rewarding. But, it was also the hardest thing I have ever done.

I asked my dad if we could schedule regular times where I could check in with him and make sure that I was doing okay. I did sin again, but it helped so much to have a mom, dad and God that would help when I had trouble. It took a while of having my conscience woken up by God so He could turn my heart toward Him and my parents again. I'm glad He did.

Intercede for your child

The only One who has the power to convict your child of sin is God. Ask God to soften your child's heart. Be sure to use your prayer closet on his behalf every day! The effective prayer of a righteous "mom" avails much. I also love Job's prayer for his grown children interceding for them just in case any of them had sinned against God.[20]

Confess

The idea of confession is to do whatever it takes to remove any stumbling blocks that we've place on the paths between everyone else and us. That doesn't mean others will ask our forgiveness for their faults if we ask for theirs, or that they'll forgive us if we ask. It doesn't even mean they'll like us! But, if we want to be a key player in encouraging someone to trust the Lord, we have to obey Him when He says, "If, therefore, you bring your gift to the altar and there remember that your brother has anything against you, leave your gift before the altar, and go your way; first be reconciled to your brother, and then come and offer your gift."[21]

We know that the wrath of "mom" doesn't accomplish the righteousness of God. We're to put away malice.[22] Confess your faults to your children and ask their forgiveness for anything you're aware of. Remember to place yourself in the other person's shoes by asking yourself, "How would I want someone who had hurt me to approach me?" This helps me to take full responsibility for my own behavior, and not justify myself with apologies that sound like, "I'm sorry I was in such a bad mood, but you know how rough it's been for me lately."

We know that confrontations and lectures don't work; they only push people further away. Jesus made it very clear that we're to do everything we can to make things right with those who are hurt by us, as well as those who hurt us. That would certainly include the members of our own household. It would also include adult children who have moved out. I sometimes teasingly refer to our older children as our "lab-rats" since they were the focus of our early child-training research. We've had to lay aside some of the teachings we received in those early days, and I've had to ask forgiveness for some of our "experiments." We want to smooth the way for them by removing as many blockages as we possibly can.

Wait

Don't look for a reciprocal response in your child if you confess your faults to him. Conviction of sin has to come from inside his own heart and mind, just as ours has to come from inside of us. Just keep obeying God and setting an example he

Preparing the Weak

can observe and follow.

And don't be consumed with looking for fruit (positive growth) in your child. Keep looking to the Lord for your own heart, "keeping your eyes on Jesus."[23] God delights in letting us see the fruit of our obedience to Him if we keep focusing on Him. If we start focusing on the fruit of our labors to see if there is more fruit, it's like watching for a pot of water to boil, or like grasping the wind. And our child will begin to feel like he's under a microscope.

Ask

Ask your child if you're doing anything that hurts or offends him. I've had to do this many times with my family and I know how hard it is. Trials of fire bring all sorts of fears and faults to the surface for everyone to see. I was surprised that one of my children had imaginary offenses against me as well as real ones. As I listened, I addressed the real ones and later found that the imaginary ones began to dry up on their own. I could tell which ones were real though – they stung with truth. The imaginary ones had no effect other than to jolt my pride just before I let them go.

> And let us not be weary in well doing, for in due season we shall reap, if we faint not.
>
> GALATIANS 6:9

Opening up to another person, particularly a parent, is risky, so our child needs to know we won't defend ourselves or react or accuse them if they open up to us. And we need to have patience if it takes a while for them to respond.

Listen

Someone asked our oldest child (whom we write about so much in our first book) what the most effective thing we did to help turn him around. He answered, "They began to listen. I felt for the first time like I was understood. It made a huge difference in our relationship with them and my response to God."

I was doing many other things at that time to try to win him back, including secret prayer for him, cutting emotional ties and confessing my faults. But listening to him was what he felt impacted him the most.

> But everyone must be quick to hear, slow to speak and slow to anger; for the anger of man does not achieve the righteousness of God.
>
> JAMES 1:19

Everyone needs someone who will listen. If we have a pattern of advising or correcting our children whenever they open up, it will take real effort to listen without automatically dispensing "good advice."

And try not to overload them with advice. When teens already know our opinion on an issue, it comes across as nagging if we keep restating it. They need to see Jesus' love in us when they know we disagree with them.

Invest in Your Marriage

Make sure your relationship with your spouse is a priority. Conflicts with children drain us moms of large amounts of resources. Couples can pool their energies to save a troubled child for short periods of time, but extended struggles wear on a marriage. If all of your in-depth conversations center on your children, or end in arguments, or if a wife is greeting her husband each night with cries for help with the children, the marriage probably needs to move to the top of the list.

Preparing the Weak

Bill insisted we get away alone for a few days each year to try to keep our marriage a priority. I went with him, but with resistance when our children were very small. I now wish I hadn't resisted – the children don't remember very much about those weekends we were away, but I will never forget them.

If your marriage is already damaged, it can seem overwhelming to focus on two major relationships at once. Don't be discouraged; just ask the Lord what He wants you to do next. You may see that you need to apply the things you're learning about winning your child's heart to your spouse. Or you may be in a very difficult place where you have done everything you can, and can only pray for your husband. Maybe your marriage is already broken. The Lord will guide you if you ask Him, but make sure you ask.

Commend Them

Don't assume your children know you're proud of them because they finished a difficult paper or went the extra mile. Tell them in a way you know they will appreciate – a note or an e-mail, a hug or a kiss, a word spoken privately or over dinner with family. Do whatever makes them comfortable and helps them to hear you. Avoid "saccharine praise" – overly commending someone for so little that they have no desire to improve, "Mother is *sooo proud* of you for making your bed this morning!"

Try Humor

See if you can deflect some tension with humor. Our sons, Daniel and Stephen, forgot their lunches for an out-of-town event, which would have forced me to buy and deliver lunches to them in the middle of my already tightly-planned day. It was hard for me to forgive them because I had warned them several times to do whatever it would take to make sure their gear and lunches were packed and loaded in the van. When the realization hit me that they'd walked happily out of the house without them and I would have to make major changes in my day, I felt like screaming. Instead, I calmly turned to them, smiled and slowly whispered, "I am now going to strangle both of you very, very slowly. Until your eyes pop out of their sockets. And they roll around on the carpet. Then I'm going to chase them down and squish them into the ground. Like this." I twisted my foot into the carpet. "And I'll keep squishing them until I start to feel better." They laughed. They knew I was saying that I wasn't happy that they didn't do what they were warned several times to do. They also knew my frustrations with them were finding a vent through humor, rather than anger. Sometimes it helps, but sometimes the frustration is just too big to deflect. But, for smaller trials, or when you feel like everything around you has just gotten too serious for too long, try humor.

I will add here that the boys had a friend who happened to be standing next to them that day who stared at me, frozen and completely speechless. If your teens aren't used to that type of humor (which I am sure still lingers from my dysfunctional background), I wouldn't recommend trying to incorporate it now. (Their friend is doing better now.)

Encourage

Project a casual you-can-do-it attitude when talking with your child. If *you* don't really believe they'll eventually make the right choice, do the right thing, or turn out all right, why should they? You'll project your disbelief to them. Out of the abundance of the heart, the mouth will (eventually) speak.[24]

Preparing the Weak

If you really don't believe they'll do well, confess those fears to the Lord in your prayer closet. Ask Him to remove any cynicism or pessimistic attitudes. A sense of warning in your spirit that your child might make a wrong choice is much different than a nagging worry or fearful, gloomy outlook. And if the concern is God-given, He provides grace and wisdom to pray.

When our son, Jon, was about twenty, he flung himself across our bed, sighed deeply and said, "I don't think I believe in the Bible anymore." I swung my chair around to face him, immediately pushing down all feelings of panic, remembering how unproductive they'd been in the past, and calmly, gently asked, "Really? Why?"

> Let your child know you believe in him, that he'll make the right decision in the end.

He then poured out his heart over the next hour about how some strongly-opinionated friends had dismissed him as being unspiritual because of his decision to attend a secular college. It had been the culmination of a year-long debate which always ended up with him feeling pushed into a corner with one Scripture or another. He couldn't prove from Scripture that he was obeying the Lord by attending this school, but neither could he reconcile their harsh "our-interpretation-is-the-only-interpretation" view with his own feelings that he was to attend it. That day, he was very discouraged, and just gave up. The Lord Jesus, whom he believed he had a good relationship with, and whom He thought had been leading him to this school, He would still cling to. The Bible, which he didn't understand as well, couldn't defend as well as his friends, and couldn't mesh with his leading, he would let go of.

Though my heart was pounding, I never said a word until he

finished. Then I softly and confidently said, "Honey, every man of God is eventually tested to find out what he really believes. Now *you're* being tested about what you really believe. I think I know the Lord well enough to believe He's going to bring you through this and show you the truth. And I think I know you well enough to know that you're going to respond to truth when you see it. How can I pray for you?"

I could see that he was feeling loved and understood (instead of being alienated and lectured as I'd been known to do in the past), so I went on, reminding him of past trials where God had helped him, and where he'd chosen truth. Even though I could remember times in the past when he *hadn't* chosen truth, I chose to remind him of the times he had. I pointed him back to Jesus to look for wisdom and help.

As soon as he left, I closed the door and practically fell on my face before God – and panicked! But, I poured my panic out to the Lord, with cries for help for my son. Bill joined me in praying for him, and I continued praying on and off over the next couple of years. Bill also had several meaningful talks with him, gently warning him not to allow bitterness or judgment to get a foothold so he wouldn't end up like the people he was encountering.

Over the next three years, we noticed our son's heart getting a little softer, his views a little more balanced, and he was reading the Bible a little more. He went on to graduate with honors from the secular college and also with honors from an online Christian law school. After graduation he sent out scads of resumes to California law firms and landed an interview. I found him packing his gear the night before he moved out, and took a few moments to tell him how much growth I'd seen in him since that conversation three years before.

"Oh, yes, that conversation," he smiled. "Yes, of course, I still believe in the Bible. I think what I learned from that experience was that God is very generous. He sends rain on the just and the unjust, and gives every good gift, even to ungenerous, or judgmental, unkind people. I figured out if I want to be like Him, I have to be generous with everyone, including people who aren't like Him."

Three years before, he'd been arguing with his friends about what he knew about God and had lost the argument. His goal had shifted to being more like the Lord, and he'd won the real battle.

When children are struggling in the waters of their own weaknesses, mistakes and sin, they can call out for help by thrashing about in the water (causing trouble). They're hoping for a life raft. If they get the message that their parents, who know and love them best, don't believe they'll make it, they'll either give up and drown or look for someone else who will believe they will make it. Let your child know you believe he'll make the right decision in the end.

Give Them Room to Make Mistakes

When Kate was 17 and getting ready for nursing school she signed up for some nursing prerequisites, and then added an elective, bringing her to fifteen credits. She'd also committed to two part-time jobs. Admittance to nursing school would be very competitive, and she'd have to keep her grades high if she hoped to get in. If she over-committed, her grades might drop. I felt she was taking on too much, and let her know. She listened, thought it over, and then decided she could handle it.

I talked it over with Bill and he encouraged me to let her make that decision, even if it meant she'd have to learn the hard way not to over-commit. I had a hard time letting it go as I watched her burn the midnight oil studying her way through the semester. On a particularly tough night of study, she smiled and said, "Mom, you *may* have been right. I may have over scheduled." My reply was a fun, "Told 'ya!" And then, "Everyone makes bad choices sometimes. I certainly have. Good for you that it was only a bad choice in your schedule." At this printing, Kate has finished school and just passed her boards.

See Them Correctly

If your child has been born again, try to view him in the more correct life-long relationship as your brother (or sister) in Christ, and less in the temporary stewardship relationship of parent-child. This shift allows very helpful truths from Scripture to come into play, such as our responsibility to a weaker brother, how to correct someone caught in sin, and the importance of loving each other as Jesus loved us.

If he's not yet born again, then it's all the more important that we demonstrate God's love to him through our own changed heart. We have the call from Jesus to be a fisher of men's hearts, and we must begin with the "men" in our own household.

Only Confess Your Own Sins

If you believe your husband is a stumbling block of offense to your child through insensitivity or harshness, or even through lax parenting and poor example, be careful not to discuss his sins with your child, or take matters into your own hands. Just confess your own sins, and try to concentrate on keeping your own heart right. Pray for your husband and child, and learn to wait on the Lord for direction. You might begin to see your husband in a new light as you pray for him, or you might receive direction to appeal to him. (Once is an appeal, repeated appeals are nagging.)

However, if there are illegal, immoral, or abuse issues (or escalating verbal abuse), you must seek outside Christian, professional, or legal help. Hiding these kinds of sins isn't "love covering a multitude of sins;" it's giving tacit consent to wrongdoing. Ask the Lord to guide you in finding help and safety for you and your child – but find help. Ask God to help you guard your heart against bitterness so you won't complicate the problem further by grieving His Spirit.

Don't be Ensnared by Unwarranted Guilt

Use guilt for what it's meant– to get free of real sin in your life – and leave the supplementary, false guilt alone. Your child received his very own post-Eden "sin chip" and his own free will upon his arrival into this universe. He won't be able to stand before God with the argument that his parents were to blame for all of his bad behavior. That's not an excuse to be a contributing factor in his sinful choices, either, remembering that Jesus said it would be better to have a millstone hung around our necks and be cast into the sea than to cause a little one to stumble. We just want to be careful not to take on their guilt for them.

Know When to Let Go

Malachi says that in the last days *God* will turn the hearts of fathers to their children and children to their fathers. If God turns our children's hearts to their fathers, we don't want to keep them for ourselves. We're supposed to turn them to the same Savior to whom we've given our own hearts. Some parents are tempted to keep their children's hearts for themselves (the family or the family business or ministry becomes an idol), or they turn their hearts over to something or someone else (a cause or mission or another person).

We've noticed that to the degree parents *require* their children's hearts to turn toward *them*, they've lost them. But as a parent turns their own heart toward the Lord, and then opens their heart toward their children, they set the stage for God to turn that child's heart to them.

When we sense our children or teens are obedient to us from the heart, it's important that we begin gently nudging them toward knowing the Lord. I say "gently nudging" because our tendency can be to start passionately pushing, "Well? Did you have your prayer time today? Did you read your Bible? Has the Lord given you a word on that topic we discussed yet?"

Passionate pushing toward the Lord can do as much damage as retaining too much control.

Accept God's Answer Whatever It Is

You may need to accept that you won't be a key player in bringing your teen or adult child to the Lord. He may still hear your voice so loud in his head that he can't hear the Lord if you're speaking. Or you may have been so negligent that he's disconnected or bitter. But all of that is past now, and the most important thing is that he does come to the Lord.

It doesn't seem that King David's heart was won or directed toward the Lord by his earthly father, yet God found him and used him greatly. [25] Moses was removed from his earthly father's home, too, but he became great a great man of God. If your teen isn't responsive to you, do what you can to restore the relationship, but also begin praying that God will send others to surround him with His unconditional love.

Gauge the Tension

It helps to take inventory of our relationships with our children, and gauge the tension between us. We need to read the signs and do our part to improve the path between us. The following chart is a guide to determining where you may stand with your child at any given time.

Heart Monitor [26]

Hearts Bound Together
We sense that our teen's heart is in fellowship with us

- Respect for us is high. Honor begins to replace blind obedience.

- Instruction is received. Emotional line between us is gently taut, sometimes tighter, sometimes looser. As they grow up, instruction diminishes and then ceases.

- Communication remains open. They can share with us about conflicts without fear of loss in the relationship. We can talk to them about their life, choices.

Hearts Growing Cold
We sense that there's a growing distance between our hearts

- Respect is deteriorating. Honor begins to slip. Some breaking of rules or wishes.

- Instruction isn't received openly. Emotional line is getting tighter (more strain). We have to pick and choose our battles.
- Communication open when talking about things they want to, strained or closed when talking about things they don't. Sometimes they open up, sometimes they don't.

Hearts in Danger
We sense we're on the verge of losing their hearts

- Respect is all but deteriorated.
- Honor is disappearing. More open disrespect. Emotional lines very tight (lots of tension).
- Instruction isn't received openly. We're not able to talk to them without reaction or conflict. Disobey instructions.
- Communication is all but shut down.

Hearts Broken
We sense we've already lost their hearts

- Respect is gone. We sense a disconnection in emotional lines. They may already be gone in heart or body (moved out).
- Apathy or cynicism replaces honor.
- Instruction is wasted. We're unable to share any truths with them. We're casting pearls before swine.[27]
- Communication shuts down, or is tense when it happens at all.

Preparing the Weak

Children with Too Much License

Once a person has experienced license, it's hard to have it taken away. In addition, sometimes a spouse will not be in agreement with the amount of protection or liberty we believe is best for our child. Unless there are truly dangerous issues that involve things illegal or immoral, I would encourage wives to try to completely accept their husband's decisions, while still praying for the Lord to give them wisdom and if needed, a change of heart. Usurping a husband's authority in the name of spirituality simply will not bear good fruit. If, however, a husband has abandoned his position of protector, a wife may find that she needs to provide protection for the sake of her children.

It is also important to keep from panic. Panic causes us to either jerk the line in too sharply or freeze in decision-paralysis. Either way, we damage or further damage our relationship with our family, which can make it even harder for them to turn to the Lord.

Start by asking the Lord to show you what to do. Be sure to follow through on anything you think He might be showing you in relation to your own heart as you wait on Him. Many of my prayers began in panic as I "tattled" on my husband or children to God, but ended in personal correction. Each time I obeyed that correction or direction, something began to improve. It began only in my own heart, but ended up bearing fruit in my family.

Here are a few questions you'll want to think about before deciding what to do.

- How much license has our child been allowed to have thus far?
- How long has he been enjoying it?

Children of Character II

- How strongly does he feel about it?
- How mature is he? Emotionally? Spiritually?
- Is his behavior so disruptive or destructive that it's damaging the rest of the family?
- Do we think he might benefit from pastoral, medical or professional help?
- Do we think he'd leave if we took away his liberties?
- How strong is the bond of love between us right now?
  - How would I do if he left?

> For whatever is born of God overcomes the world; and this is the victory that has overcome the world - our faith. Who is the one who overcomes the world, but he who believes that Jesus is the Son of God?
>
> 1 John 5:4-5

As you pray and wait on the Lord, you may sense that you need to work on your relationship with your child before you remove a liberty. Or you may realize it would be best to pull in the reins on just one liberty, and overlook the rest as you begin to try to regain his heart. Or perhaps you'll see it's right to remove all his liberties at once. You might see that there are medical, physical, mental or emotional problems that need more experienced or professional help. You may even need to ask an unrepentant older teen or adult child move out, especially if there are immoral or illegal issues.

Even if you are under good family counseling or professional counseling about the situation, be sure to look to the Lord for guidance. There are many different ways He can lead. But He is the only One who truly knows your child, and He can help one step at a time as you lean on Him. His answer for you might be different than what other parents might do. It might be

Preparing the Weak

different than the way He led you for other children. The only way you'll know for sure what to do is to *truly* ask Him. God delights in sincere prayers from His children who want to follow His direction.

The parents of an out-of-control ten year-old realized they'd granted her far too many liberties for her maturity level. Her behavior was disruptive and rude both inside and outside the home, but removing her from the few activities she was already involved in was difficult for them. At first, they felt as if they would be unduly punishing their daughter and isolating her from safe and productive environments if they eliminated her outside activities until her behavior improved. They also felt she'd never be motivated to behave better if they took everything away.

This sweet, loving couple viewed liberty as a treat (or a carrot), rather than a natural progression of maturing behavior. They needed to see maturity itself as a reward and liberties as natural byproducts of maturity.

As they prayed for direction they began to warm to the idea of bringing her completely home from outside-the-home activities, back under their wing. This decision required the mother to cut her own extra activities as well to give her attention more fully to their weak daughter. Listen to her testimony.

> "One thing that has come about by my pulling myself out of outside ministry and other responsibilities is that I have had to come face-to-face with the realities of my life, such as where I get my fulfillment, the conditions of all my children's hearts, the state of my marriage, and my own character. It hasn't looked very pretty. But we have really been making some strides in these areas, especially in our marriage.
>
> Since I've been staying home, God has been quite

faithful to show the lack of respect I had for my husband that I never knew was there. It was deeply rooted in my life as I fed and watered it daily. I have also been greatly convicted of unbelief, pride and prayerlessness in some areas.

I don't know what else to say except that repentance is a good thing. I have enjoyed such freedom and joy in carrying out what my husband wants for our family. The excess weight and stress is off my shoulders and on his. Another plus to my giving back the leadership of our home to my husband has been that he is much more involved with the children, which is great to see. Not that he wasn't before, but now it is different and better.

> Since I've been staying home, God has been quite faithful to show the lack of respect I had for my husband that I never knew was there.

Our daughter has still been difficult, but I haven't had this kind of hope - *that I will be okay regardless of her behavior* - since she was born. Her conduct seems less major now compared to the growth, pain, joy, forgiveness and humbling that has been occurring in our home. I can't describe the freedom I am experiencing right now as I have been confessing and surrendering things to God."

These parents thought of removing liberties as isolation or punishment, which made it hard to implement. But, the real picture was that they needed to pull their weak and stumbling daughter back in under their wing to protect her from riding her wobbly bike into traffic because she had convinced them that she needed to be there to be happy and whole.

Preparing the Weak

These parents have been asking the Lord for mercy and a quick work in their daughter's heart, while also preparing their own hearts to do "whatever it takes" to reach her. They're now, less than a year later, seeing tiny buds of fruit:

> "We have had some good breakthroughs with our daughter. One day last week, she had another huge blow-up and was screaming everything she could think at me. I had unbelievable peace through the whole thing. This is so unlike me, and something I can only attribute to the ongoing work of grace in my heart. My gentle response allowed the situation to end with her in my arms, reading Scripture and praying together. She then confessed something she had done when she was nine! I would never have experienced this tender outcome to one of her tantrums had I still been an on-the-go mom as the world (and my church) has told me I should be."

It's easy for our children to stall in the mode of being takers with attitudes that say, "What's in this activity for me? What will I gain from it? What can I do that will please or benefit me?" If we parents also view liberties in the same way thinking, "What will my child gain from this activity? What advantages will my child receive?" it will be nearly impossible for us to withdraw them because we'll view their removal as a *loss of potential benefits*, rather than a *gain of godly protection*. And our children will emulate our own wrong thinking.

Ask the Lord to help you see if your children have too many liberties. If you receive direction to pull them back under your wing, explain to them in a gentle setting that you've erred in your decision-making and that you see now you need to bring them back home for a while. Humbly ask their forgiveness. Use this time to confess any hurts you may have caused. The more sincere they see you are, the easier these new laws will be to accept.

When our children's thinking begins to change to doing what's right rather than what they want, maturity will begin to sprout, and the whole world will gradually open up to them. The opportunities to be a light outside the home are inexhaustible.

Children Who are Over-Controlled

What if your child hasn't been given the liberties he should have? Teens who've been granted too few liberties can be hard to spot on the surface. They can look like "model Christians" – happy, compliant, diligent. They may very much like having their decisions made for them. Strong external rules can make some teens feel safe, and being told what to do (or what someone else thinks God wants you to do) is certainly easier than finding the Lord's direction for yourself and learning to make wise decisions on your own. That immature mindset is very much like the Israelites' attitude when they begged Moses to speak for God so they wouldn't have to risk having Him speak directly to them.[28]

It can be difficult for young people who've had most of their decisions made for them to sense God's voice in their spirit over their parents' voice in their head. If they've been told that their parents are supposed to control them into adulthood, they may believe that any kind of independence (even healthy, independent self-government) would be a form of rebellion. For these teens, forming an opinion from

> Some over-controlled teens like having decisions made for them.

the Scriptures that's even slightly different than their parents or church leaders is risky. Forming and expressing their own beliefs or convictions might also risk losing the respect and approval of parents, family, friends or church family. They might even lose financial support or even be excommunicated from the family or church if they don't agree with their parents. They quickly learn not to "rock the boat" if they don't want to find themselves on the outside looking in.

Even if they sense something is amiss, if being controlled is the only system they've ever known, they may strongly hold to it and defend it. Losing the security of being told what to do is scary. It's not uncommon for such young people to faithfully obey their parents on the outside while feeling directionless and frustrated on the inside. Those who are truly born again are weak Christians, indeed, because they've been allowed to remain emotionally and spiritually dependent.

Some over-controlled teens and young adults go in the opposite direction and look like rebels. They feel heavy from parental, family or supposed Biblical expectations. They often feel like they're stagnating or suffocating or perishing. They might feel they can never please their parents no matter how hard they try. These young people grow tired of being so tightly controlled and begin to yank on that taut line between them and their parents. Sometimes it's a gradual tension over years, or it may just show up during arguments, or sometimes it's an unexpected explosion that shocks everyone – even the young person. Their behavior looks like rebellion, which unfortunately causes controlling parents to tighten the line even more, sometimes going to drastic measures, which, in turn, cause their hurting child to pull away even more.

Even if a teen grows up in an over-controlling home without any signs of outward rebellion, that doesn't mean things are as they should be. Because young people from over-controlling environments don't receive training or practice in how to make wise decisions on their own, it's not uncommon for them to have trouble making decisions, or they make bad decisions when they're finally on their own. They often make unwise friendships and relationship choices. Or they continue to yield to their parents' decisions, perhaps in finances, friendships, and maybe even in marriage, and then enter marriage or a career unprepared for personal communication. They can have trouble handling money, and unless their parents or new spouse rescue them, they often crash and burn. It's a rare young person who can recognize his parents' error and commit to honor them, while also obeying what he believes the Lord is leading him to do. We've known very few.

It should be obvious to us as parents that if we have to resort to external controls with older children and teens, something is wrong. God wants all His children, which includes us parents and our teens, to be controlled by His Spirit.[29] The letter (external rules and controls) kills. The Spirit gives life.[30] Laws *are* needed for the lawless (very young and immature). But, as the very young grow up and the immature become more mature, we're not supposed to remain planted at the helm of control in their lives. The Lord is supposed to be taking over our temporary time in that position.

> It should be obvious to us as parents that if we have to resort to external controls with older children and teens, something is wrong.

Sometimes, parents are the last to see there is a problem. And sometimes it's the child who is unwilling to admit there's a problem because it feels too risky to begin trusting in the Lord. If you think you may err on the side of over-control, here are a few questions you may want to ask.

Preparing the Weak

- Is our child compliant because he's obeying God from the heart, or because he feels he must agree with us in order to please God?
- If we removed some of the rules, do we think he'd continue to walk in obedience to God and his own conscience?
- Could our child be rebelling because we control him too tightly?
- Do I feel fearful when our child fails or makes a mistake or sins?
- Have I ever used the Bible as a threat or a weapon?
- How would we feel if our teen came to different conclusions when he read the Scriptures?
- Do we believe our child can discuss his views with us? With me?
- Does our child believe he can discuss his views with us? With me?
- Do we believe we listen and care about his feelings?
- Does our child believe we listen and care about his feelings?
- What happened the last time he shared a differing view with us? With me?
- Do we punish our child emotionally, or cut him off if he doesn't agree or comply?
- Do we ever use financial pressure or other means to control him?

> Our teen and adult children have lived with us long enough and interacted with us enough times to already know our opinions (and usually quite well) about certain behaviors.

- Is my view of my child largely as a parent, or do I also relate to him as my younger brother or sister in Christ?
- Do I ever put myself into our child's shoes? If I did, would I sense that I was loved and understood?

If a teen is already in open rebellion, such as defiantly breaking reasonable house rules, experimenting with drugs or alcohol, breaking the law or becoming involved in an immoral relationship, we would, of course, need to explain and enforce certain consequences, which may include moving out. However, those consequences would need to be enforced for our child's benefit, not our home's benefit. Our goal needs to be to restore our child with the least amount of damage to other persons – not to preserve our home, or our image of what our home should be.

If a child has moved out and is living in immorality, God still calls us to love him. It's true that Paul scolded the Corinthians for accepting immorality within the church and then acting as though it was acceptable. Love doesn't condone immoral behavior. Removing someone from the church, however, doesn't mean we treat him with negative or cool emotions, or cut off all communication. It means we treat him like someone who is not really a Christian – as one who is in need of truth and love, not as one who is already walking in truth.

Our teen and adult children have lived with us long enough and interacted with us enough times to already know our opinions (and usually quite well) about certain behaviors. If we can still be loving and accepting to them, while not condoning or supporting their behavior, this is love indeed. But if we tend to ostracize people when they don't do what we want or expect them to, or do what we believe God wants or expects them to, it creates a greater divide that will need to be crossed later. We must show love to people who don't obey God while obeying

Preparing the Weak

God ourselves. Jesus saved some of His strongest rebukes for religious people who cut others off when they failed.

If you see that your child hasn't been granted liberties he should have, confess that to him and ask for his forgiveness. If you gain a new understanding of the Scriptures, or of your role as a parent, and you see that your former understanding caused damage, explain that too, and ask for forgiveness. Be sincere, humble and open. Ask the Lord for wisdom on how to get those training wheels off as safely as possible. Some children never want to take their training wheels off! Ask the Lord to begin speaking to your child, calling him to Himself, while you try to give him a little more liberty.

> Weaknesses, temptations and sins our children are drawn toward are often the same ones that have trapped us in the past.

Conclusion

It helps to remember that the weaknesses, temptations and sins our children are drawn toward are often the same ones that trapped us in the past, and may sometimes still appeal to our own nature. It's also a little easier to have patience in their maturing process if we can see our children as our younger, weaker brothers and sisters in Christ (or our future brothers and sisters in Christ), and not simply as *our* children. This correct view can help us not to take their sins so personally.

Maturity can take longer for some than others. No matter where our children are in maturity or liberty, God can help guide us to the next step. Ask Him for wisdom and grace

CHAPTER THREE:

Lifting Protections as our Children Mature ~ Working Ourselves Out of a Job

When children begin to make strides in personal self-government, we want to encourage them. To keep them under strong parental rule when they're beginning to rule themselves rightly would be wrong, and would discourage further growth. It would be similar to jogging next to them each time they rode their bikes, even though they no longer needed training wheels (or us) to help them balance. The time to jog next to them is when they're *learning* to ride. But, once we see they're getting their balance, we need to let them begin riding on their own.

It's easy to understand how attached we parents can become to jogging next to our children's bicycles, especially if we keep focusing on how hard the cement is. But, it's very important to understand how frustrating it would be to have someone constantly jogging next to you making sure you didn't fall even though you could ride. That picture says more about the jogger than the rider.

Young people are going to fall when they start to ride on their own. Everyone does. Even a righteous man "falls seven times" and rises again. Part of learning to ride is learning to fall and get back up again.

It's frustrating for anyone to make strides in improvement, but continue to be micromanaged. One has only to read the comic strip *Dilbert* to see how quickly micromanagement produces resignation and cynicism. Our goal is to bring the weak to maturity so they'll be able to stand firm in the world without us. They are to shine as lights in a dark world, not always clustered together with all the other lights.

Nearly all men can stand adversity, but if you want to test a man's character, give him power.
ABRAHAM LINCOLN

Children of Character II

It's important that we learn how to loosen parental rules (training wheels), one small, earned notch at a time, so they'll gradually gain the strength and confidence they need when it's time to take off.

Stephen (who is seventeen at this printing) was seven when we told him he couldn't play at the neighbor's home any longer. Here is his perspective.

> FROM STEPHEN: When my parents told me I wouldn't be able to play at my friend's house, I was disappointed. I knew my friend was doing things he shouldn't, but I didn't feel like he would change if I said something. I also knew if I told my parents about it, they wouldn't let me go over there anymore. I really enjoyed getting to play with him and I knew I'd miss seeing him.
>
> When I was nine, my parents let me play trumpet in a Christian band program. Before I joined, they took me aside and told me I'd have to do what was right no matter what anyone else was doing or I wouldn't be allowed to go back. I really enjoyed band and wanted to keep going, so I did what was right.
>
> When I was thirteen, I wanted to join the Civil Air Patrol Cadet Program (CAP). My parents knew it wasn't a Christian program, but said they saw I was doing what was right in a Christian group and thought I was ready to keep doing what was right in a non-

---
I do not ask you to take them out of the world, but to keep them from the evil one. As You have sent me into the world, I also have sent them into the world.

JOHN 17:15, 18

Lifting Protections as Our Children Mature

Christian group. They gave me the same rule that if I couldn't do what was right no matter what everybody else was doing, I wouldn't be allowed to go back. I was excited to join CAP because I enjoy flying. I was also looking forward to doing what I knew God wanted me to no matter who was around. My parents' confidence in me that I would do right made me want to live up to their expectations.

I did well in CAP, and my parents let me work for a week in our state legislature 150 miles from home. They told me if I did what was right when I was that far away, I could go back the next year.

When I was fourteen I asked if I could go to a weeklong CAP boot camp four hours away. They weren't sure if I should go at first, but told me later they prayed about it and thought I was ready. I was so glad. I really felt it was God's will for me to go. I knew there wouldn't be many Christian cadets there, so I prayed that God would help me be a light for Him. He did. I got to share my faith in Jesus with four other cadets.

At fifteen, I went to Honduras on my first mission trip without my parents. And when I was sixteen I went to Ecuador twice on mission trips. God taught me so many lessons on those trips. I'm so glad I could go.

> I see that my parents cared more about me than their relationship with their neighbors.
>
> Stephen Freeman

Now when I think about that day when my parents made me come home from my friend's house, I see that they cared more about me than their relationship with the neighbors. That really means a lot to me now.

Stephen's character eventually grew. He went from weakness to strength, and then from strength to strength.

- Weak - being influenced to do wrong (demonstrated when he hid his sin and his friend's sin from us)
- Stronger – doing what was right no matter what anyone else was doing (demonstrated weekly in a Christian band program and in a squadron that had a large percentage of Christian cadets)
- Stronger – influencing unsaved peers for Jesus (at a boot camp with very few Christians)
- Stronger – serving the needy and sharing the gospel on the mission field

To have let Stephen play at the neighbors' house when he wasn't mature, or to have let him stay in band or CAP if he wasn't standing alone would have been under-protection. To have kept him from going to boot camp or on mission trips when he was ready would have been over-protection.

The Corinthian church turned a blind eye to idolatrous and immoral church members and stumbled with jealousy, division, lawsuits, selfishness and gross immorality. Paul warned those weak believers to separate themselves from immoral people *within* their own church body.[31]

In a few short years our teens will be navigating on their own in a world of unfiltered Internet access and dangerous people. It's not about who we associate with, but about knowing and obeying Jesus.[32] As an adult, our Savior spent so much of his time with "gluttons and sinners" that he was accused of being a winebibber. We need to make sure our children understand that the Bible warns us not about not associating with the world, but about loving the world (conforming to it, approving of its ways).

CHAPTER FOUR:

Parental Idols and Their Consequences

Nevertheless, with most of them God was not well-pleased. For they were laid low in the wilderness. Now these things happened as examples for us...1 Corinthians 10:5, 6

I was never very good at identifying with Israel's idol worship when I read through the Old Testament. After all, I've never been tempted to burn incense on a hill, sacrifice my children to Moloch, or hide statues in my saddlebag. I always thought there should have been no doubt in any of their minds that they were playing with fire, and that it was a bad thing to do.

But the New Testament tells us that the Old Testament is supposed to be an example to us[33] so we don't have to repeat Israel's painful mistakes. (Bill and I get to thinking about that purpose each time we hear Old Testament customs and laws being resurrected in ways that replace New Testament grace. But, I digress...). Anyway, I got to thinking: *How am I supposed to relate to all of Israel's romps with idol worship? No one I know bows down to idols.*

And then I got to thinking that God dealt with Israel in very physical, outward ways that could be seen with their eyes – fire in the bush, physical plagues in Egypt, parting of the sea, cloud by day, fire by night, physical blessings for obedience, physical cursings for disobedience and so on.

Move into the New Testament and Jesus goes beyond outward behavior and deals straight with the heart. He tells us that if we *look* at someone lustfully we've committed adultery in our hearts, if we're angry with a brother we're guilty of murder, if we do everything right on the outside, even to the extent of giving away our house with all its stuff (including that new wheat grinder, all those scrapbook supplies, and that gorgeous antique table), live the rest of our lives out in some, poor, forgotten corner of the world, and then die a painful, gory martyr's death while never recanting our faith, but we didn't have love as the reason behind our sacrifice, then we have, and are, nothing. Zeroes. Losers. First Corinthians 13 is a pretty strong sermon on the motivation of the heart.

So, if the New Testament points us to the Old as an example, it would seem there must be *heart issues* in those accounts of idol worship that I need to see with eyes of understanding. (Yes, I know, pretty simple stuff, but I can be a little slow.)

I now see that Israel's continuous pull toward idols was due to a hollow that was carved in the center of her heart that God made to be filled with Himself. When God *was* at the center of Israel's heart she was blessed and thrived; when she let Him slip from center, idols seeped into the void. Israel's heart couldn't remain empty if God slid out. As with the nature of hearts, it had to be filled with *something*. And she didn't often keep God in the center.

That's too bad. Poor Israel. What a sad state of affairs for her. Wait. I'm supposed to be learning a lesson by example here.

Going on, I ask myself: Even though Israel let idols slip in, did she still have a relationship with her God? Not a great one, but yes, she did. In her compromised relationship, did she still seek His provision? Yes, even to the point of whining for those yummy leeks she left in Egypt. And even though things weren't completely right between her and God, did she still seek His favor? She did. His protection? Of course. But what about God Himself? Did she make any concerted efforts to keep God in the center of her heart? Not very often. Hmm, I can sense myself nervously, mentally shifting and pacing. I begin to hope there are no lessons in here for me after all.

I then ask: With what did Israel fill her heart whenever her God started to slip from it? The answer seems to be – with

Parental Idols and Their Consequences

whatever was nearby. And the two influences that were nearby were the world (the cultures surrounding her) and her kinsmen (those twelve million or so 24/7 fellow-sojourners who kept making unwise, peer-dependent decisions).

Now I'm getting a little closer to home. According to Merriam-Webster, the definition of an idol is:

1. representation or symbol of object of worship
2. a likeness of something
3. a form or appearance visible but without substance
4. <u>an object of extreme devotion</u>
5. a false conception

Spiritually expanding that definition, what if we said that an idol could be *anything* that sits in God's rightful place in the center of our hearts? What if it were anything that we begin to cherish more than our relationship with Him? What if idols were things, even *good things* that we begin to think longingly about, or desire or love or treasure even a *smidgen* more than God Himself?

Now here is my lesson through the example of the Old Testament: Idols are alive and well! I know

> When did those good causes God called me to do move from being something I did for Him…to how I defined myself?

because I suddenly recognize a few people and causes I've allowed to crowd out the love and affection that I was supposed to devote to God. When did they move to the center of my heart and begin to define my focus? When did those good causes God called me to do move from being something I did for Him…to how I defined myself?

And what about those passionate issues I've picked up from a few of my kinsmen? Perhaps defending my faith or convictions has become more of a passion to me than simply knowing the Lord more deeply. Or getting my understanding of an issue or the Scriptures across to someone more important than letting myself be misunderstood and just resting in the Lord? Perhaps I see that I look down on people who don't agree with me, or become offended when they don't take up the causes that I hold dear.

LESSONS ON IDOLS

I've learned a few things about idols over the years. I wish I could say these insights came from observations of immature Christians I've met over the years. Alas, I took many of them out of my own journal.

- Idols rarely look ugly, unpleasant or unjustified. Who would cherish an ugly, unpleasant, worthless rival over a loving relationship with the living God? No, they're attractive. They can even look irresistible. Or cute or adorable or needy. Like a puppy.
- Idols tend to start out small. Also like a puppy.
- There seems to be a never-ending supply of unclaimed idols frolicking about the curb of the path of Life – not unlike stray puppies.
- Idols like to whine at us for attention.
- If we're not moving forward on the path God is leading us, idols somehow find their way onto the doorsteps of our hearts. (Resting in the Lord is moving forward, like resting on an escalator; resisting the Holy Spirit is camping on our issues.)

Parental Idols and Their Consequences

- Idols can look hungry and needy and like they will die if we don't take care of them.
- Idols don't go away on their own.
- Idols can project guilt through a closed door.
- Idols lead us to believe they'll go away if we feed them just once.
- Idols lie.
- Idols dart in if we open the door of our hearts even a crack to them.
- Idols instinctively know how to find the warm, soft rug in front of the hearth where the hottest fires of our hearts are blazing.
- If they find any empty spot there, idols curl up and get very comfortable.
- Even when they're sleeping, idols are alive and growing.
- Idols don't like to budge once they find that soft, warm place.
- Idols eventually grow into attack dogs – with teeth.
- Idols show teeth and attitude if they feel threatened. Sometimes we don't even know they're in the house until someone comes along and happens to kick them. Then they start barking and growling. Funny thing – it sounds almost as though *we* are barking and growling. (It sounds like that to our family or friends, too.)

Alright, enough of canine analogies. The point is that our hearts can hide idols well, which makes them pretty hard to spot. At least, our own idols are for us hard to spot. Other people's

Children of Character II

can be quite easy.

My own idols can look and feel more like a cause that's gotten out of proportion. Or they can start out as a diversion, a justification, a temptation or a belief. Idols can dress themselves up in church clothes so they look like righteous indignation or strong convictions or high standards or a new revelation or teaching. When a good purpose begins to drive me, I'm no longer being led by the Lord. We're not supposed to be purpose-driven, but Spirit-led.

Godly causes are godly things when they stay in their proper places; when they slide to the center of our hearts they become bad. The important thing to remember is that no matter how worthy or godly our activities look, if they're moving into the center of our hearts, becoming more important to us than our personal relationship with God and our relationships with other people, if we begin viewing most of our relationships through the spectrum of how they line up with our cause, they're developing into idols.

> We're not supposed to be purpose-driven, but Spirit-led.

If we take a look at our culture, the temptations are as obvious as they were for Israel: wealth, greed, immorality, vanity, materialism and power to name a few. Even good gifts from God like simple pleasures, personal fulfillment, a great job or happiness can trip us up if they become very, very important to us. If we let our own interests slide into God's rightful place in our heart then we'll be driven to be (or get) newer, nicer, bigger, more, prettier, lovelier, more powerful and upgraded everythings. Our homes, possessions, careers or professions begin to become our central focus. Or our financial status, connections or affiliations. And still we never feel satisfied. Worldly idols are fairly easy for us Christians to spot. They're sleek-looking Greyhounds with shiny collars or fancy

Parental Idols and Their Consequences

poodles with neat sweaters. It just depends on our tastes.

It's a little harder to identify idols that we might be carrying around with our kinsmen, i.e. the church. Our Christian idols can look so – well, spiritual. So righteous-cause and non-idol like. So Christian. Sort of cute-puppy like. But my, my, can they bite if they get kicked. (I'm not writing from theory.)

If the definition of an idol is:

…anything that sits in God's rightful place in the center of our hearts, or anything that we cherish more than our relationship with Him, or good things that we think longingly about, or treasure more than God …

…then, does that mean that doing good works in Jesus' Name could become an idol? What about, say, community service or political action? What if we were doing it to bring about righteousness? What if we were saving lives? Could those good things become idols?

Could the family become an idol? Could our own family become an idol? What about our belief about how many children we think we should have? Our thoughts about how many children we think other people should have? What about our dress? Or music? Our health? Nutrition? The kinds of food we eat or don't eat? The kinds of food we think other Christians should eat or not eat? Could our children's education become an idol? Our feelings about our church or its programs or size or outreach or social flavor? Our own ministry or outreach? The number of people or kind of people we're reaching? What about raising godly children? What about our children themselves? Could they become more important than our relationship with God? What about our interpretations of Scripture? What about the Bible itself? Can the Bible become an idol, a message that we study, memorize, quote, defend and protect – without ever letting it judge the intentions of our own hearts? God's word is good and the Pharisees studied, memorized, quoted, defended and protected it – but they never saw Jesus.

For the word of God is living and active and sharper than any two-edged sword, and piercing as far as the division of soul and spirit, of both joints and marrow, and able to judge the thoughts and intentions of the heart. Rom 4:12

Dying to Good Desires (as well as Wrong Desires) in Order to Know Christ

Every single person who wants to grow and come to maturity in Jesus will have to experience both the death to wrong desires (sin) as well as the death to good desires (desires to do good works for Him) apart from the desire of just knowing and loving Jesus. Paul had to die to his well-earned good reputation even within the church to know Jesus. We, too, have to be willing die to everything, whether "good" or "bad" in order to follow Him. This is what our children need to see to become followers of Christ. They need to be shown how to live by watching Christians live, to learn how to crucify the flesh by watching Christians crucify the flesh. We are those Christians. We parents must be willing to die to even the good things we want for our children, so that those good hopes don't turn into idols, and then drive us.

> They need to be shown how to live by watching Christians live, to learn how to crucify the flesh by watching Christians crucify the flesh. We are those Christians.

This is a hard lesson for me. When I turn to serve only the Lord, I have joy and peace, and bear good fruit. When I forget and turn back to serving causes, even a good cause such as raising godly children, and begin to

Parental Idols and Their Consequences

make it the goal of my life, I stumble again.

Once idols are in place, they filter our view. We begin to see everything and everyone (especially those closest to us) through the filter of whatever we cherish. Some filters block out other people's good intentions (so we wrongly accuse or blame), some cover bad intentions (and we smile and say love is "blind," or fervently state, "My child/husband/friend would never…,"). It just depends on which idols we've let in and how important they are to us.

But they all cause distortion and then pain whenever we bump into those around us in our spiritual blindness. Two good questions to ask ourselves about any of the good things in our lives are:

- How do I respond when people kick them?
- How would I react if I lost them tomorrow?

IDOLS DECEIVE US

Christian values and good works can quickly become idols if they begin to replace God's rightful place in the center of our hearts. The following list[34][35] is not exhaustive. We humans can stuff more idols into a heart than pen and paper can record. But it has a few of the harder-to-spot ones that have slipped into my own heart before. See if you can recognize any that have slipped into yours.

The Idol Called Home
If the Home moves into the center of our hearts

- The **Home** enjoys an elevated status and becomes the haven from the world. The home becomes the filter through which we read the Bible. ✿ The

Perfect Home becomes the ideal, and creating the perfect home becomes our mission in life. ⚜ The enemy is anyone who threatens our ideal or hinders our pursuit of the perfect home. Sometimes outside-the-home activities or ventures that disrupt the home become the enemy.

- **Family** members are key players in preserving the home. Keeping family members at home, having Dad work from home, creating family businesses that operate from home become absolute priority. Keeping the home intact trumps financial, educational, social or spiritual needs of family members.

- **Children** become a resource to fulfill needs of the home to keep it running smoothly and in order, to the detriment of children's personal needs for more nurturing, time and attention.

- **Personal Convictions** and **Standards** center around the preservation of all things related to home, creating the perfect home, defending and preserving the home, or home life.

- The **Church** is primarily a resource to support and strengthen the home or home life.

- Outside-the-home **Ministry** takes a back seat to needs to keep the home center. Ministry takes place from home, or strengthens the home. Ministry can't intrude into home life.

- **A Worthy Cause** is the preservation, protection, promotion, strengthening, defense of the home. ⚜ Is doable if it doesn't disrupt the home.

Parental Idols and Their Consequences

- **God** is seen as the source of our cause to protect the home. He is seen primarily as Someone who wants to bless, strengthen and protect our homes.

The Idol Called Family
If the Family moves into the center of our hearts

- **Home** becomes a place to strengthen the family. Needs to keep the family intact trump needs of the home.

- The **Perfect Family** becomes our ideal. Creating and maintaining the perfect family becomes our mission in life. ✿ Patriarchal position enjoys an elevated status, often taking God's place in bestowing blessing, direction or release to family members. ✿ Beliefs about the order and role of family become the filter through which we read the Bible. ✿ The enemy is anyone who threatens our ideal, challenges our beliefs about its importance, or hinders the promotion of our beliefs or our pursuit of the perfect or "Biblical" family.

- **Children** are planned, limited, or aborted to preserve whatever our ideal picture is of the perfect family. ✿ Children enlarge, serve, bless, strengthen or live for the betterment and promotion of the family. ✿ Older or adult children are cut off if they rebel or fail in order to preserve the perfect family. Keeping family unit intact trumps children's needs for individual attention, nurturing or discipline.

- **Personal Convictions** and **Standards** about family draw heavily from popular worldly culture. ୠ Personal convictions and standards about family draw heavily from popular Christian culture, or Old Testament commands to the nation of Israel. Convictions center around the preservation of all things related to family, the perfect family, or building a strong family.

- **Church** is a resource for supporting and strengthening the family. Church is a safe place for families to work and serve. Church activities must be family-oriented to participate.

- **Ministry/Missions** are resources to strengthen the family. Must be done though, or with, or to benefit the family.

- A **Worthy Cause** is the preservation, protection, promotion, strengthening, defense of the family.

- **God** is seen as the source of our cause to protect the family. He is seen primarily as Someone who wants to bless, strengthen and protect families.

The Idol Called Children
If Children move into the center of our hearts

- **Home** becomes centered around children. Children's unrestrained sins disrupts/erodes home life. ୠ Children's gifts or strengths (and the desire to improve them) drive, disrupt/erode home life.

Parental Idols and Their Consequences

- **Family** is for receiving and training children. Needs of children trump needs of parents or others.
- **Children** enjoy an elevated status, and having children becomes our mission in life. Raising **Perfect Children** becomes the ideal, and our mission in life. Beliefs about children become the filter through which we read the Bible. The enemy is anyone who threatens our children, thwarts their progress, challenges or disagrees with our beliefs about children or hinders our pursuit of raising perfect children.
- **Personal Convictions** and **Standards** relate to the status of children.
- **Church** is a place to equip parents to train and protect their children, a place to minister to children or a resource where children can safely serve.
- **Ministry** is limited to what can be done with or around children. Ministry is primarily a resource where children can gain something. Should minister to children, or assist parents with their children.
- A **Worthy Cause** is worthy if it protects and defends children, or agrees with my belief about children.
- **God** is seen as the source of our beliefs about children. He is seen primarily as Someone who wants to bless, strengthen and protect children.

The Idol Called Personal Convictions or Standards Based on Non-foundational Issues
If Personal Convictions or Standards move into the center of our hearts

- **Home** is a place to exercise convictions with full control, a place to create a model of our ideal.
- **Family** *must* conform to our conviction or standards.
- **Children** *must* conform to our convictions or standards.
- **Personal Convictions** or **Standards** are elevated to a status nearly equal with the Bible. Sharing our convictions becomes our mission in life rather than sharing the gospel or our personal testimony. Standards become more important than love. The enemy is anyone who disagrees with our convictions or promotes an opposing view of our standards.
- **Church** is unacceptable unless it agrees with and promotes our personal convictions or standards.
- **Ministry** is as a medium to spread our personal convictions or standards.
- **Worthy Causes** are worthy if they agree with or promote and defend our personal convictions or standards.
- **God** is seen as the source of our standards and convictions. He is seen primarily as Someone who is described by our convictions and standards.

Parental Idols and Their Consequences

The Idol Called Church
If Church moves into the center of our hearts

- **Home** is secondary to church life, a "pit stop" between church activities. Needs at church trump needs at home.
- **Family** is a resource to strengthen and build the church and its ministries. Needs of church trump family needs.
- **Children** are objects of ministry, resources for service, the mark of a successful church. Needs at church trump children's needs for nurturing, attention or training.
- **Personal Convictions** or **Standards** are valuable as they relate to church doctrine, or building a strong church. Personal standards and convictions must agree with church doctrine, and members must embrace them to maintain close fellowship.
- **Church** activities and church calendar enjoy elevated status taking precedence over individual needs. Church becomes a refuge, or our entire social life. ଓ The pursuit of the **Perfect Church** becomes the ideal. Creating, finding or maintaining the perfect church becomes our mission in life. ଓ Church leadership enjoys elevated status, sometimes replacing God in giving direction and blessing to its members. ଓ The church's position or powers become the filter through which we read the Bible. The enemy is anyone who threatens our church, its doctrine, image, status-quo, unanimity,

beliefs about its role or hinders our pursuit of the perfect church.
- **Ministry** is valuable if it gets church members active in local church.
- **Worthy Causes** can't take members' time away from church activities. Causes are valuable if they make the church function better.
- **God** is seen primarily as Someone who wants to bless, strengthen and protect the church.

The Idol Called Ministry
If Ministry moves into the center of our hearts

- **Home** is secondary to ministry, a "pit stop" for R&R between ministry work. Ministry needs trump home needs.
- **Family** is a resource to help with ministry. Needs of ministry usually trump family needs.
- **Children** are a resource to help with ministry. Children should not hamper ministry. Needs of ministry usually trump children's needs.
- **Personal Convictions** and **Standards** are valuable as they relate to health of ministry, sometimes taking second place to progress of ministry.
- **Church** primarily as a resource to strengthen or enhance ministry.
- Our **Ministry** becomes our passion. Promoting our ministry becomes our mission in life. Ministry leaders enjoy elevated status as ministry leader, receiving preferential treatment or star status, lending to a

disconnection from personal accountability. Ministry is superior to ministry of the church. Beliefs about the importance of our ministry become the filter through which we read the Bible. The enemy is anyone who threatens our ministry, challenges its importance, or hinders the promotion of our ministry.

- A **Worthy Cause** is worthy if it relates to or strengthens our ministry.
- **God** as Someone whose main mission is to bless, strengthen and help with our ministry.

The Idol Called a Worthy Cause
If a Worthy Cause moves into the center of our hearts

- **Home** as secondary to our cause, a "pit stop" for R&R while working on our cause. The cause begins to trump home needs.
- **Family** members are seen as resources to strengthen or enhance our cause. The cause begins to trump family needs.
- **Children** are seen as resources to help with our cause; their needs are less important than our cause. The cause begins to trump children's needs
- **Personal Convictions** and **Standards** as valuable as they relate to promotion of our cause, sometimes taking second place to progress of our cause.
- **Church** primarily as a resource to promote our cause.

- **Ministry** is worthy if it promotes our cause.
- A **Worthy Cause** becomes our passion. It's the only cause worth working for. Promoting or defending our cause becomes our mission in life. Leaders sometime take on martyr status. Our cause is superior to other causes or ministries in the church, and becomes the filter through which we read the Bible. The enemy is anyone who threatens our cause, challenges its importance, or hinders its promotion.
- **God** is seen as the source of our passion for our cause. He is seen primarily as Someone who wants to bless, strengthen and protect our cause.

The One True God
If God is at the center of our hearts

- **Home** is the place where God is invited, the place where worship begins, where we practice loving others. Family members feel refreshed and physically and emotionally safe.
- **Family** is seen as a gift from God. Our family becomes our "neighbors" we are to love as ourselves.
- **Children** are a stewardship from God we are to love, nurture and admonish in the Lord. They are the weaker brothers and sisters for whom we lay aside some of our freedoms, our future brothers and sisters in Christ.
- **Personal Convictions** and **Standards** are personal responses to the Lord's Voice to us through His Spirit and Word.

- **Church** is a place where we gather to worship God, and train and edify one another. A place to serve as directed by the Lord.

- **Ministry** is worthy as it relates to eternity. A place to serve as directed by the Lord. Our central focus of devotion and conversation is about God and His attributes as they relate to the ministry.

- **Worthy Cause** is worthy as it relates to eternity. A place to contribute as led by the Lord. Our central focus of devotion and conversation is about God and His attributes as they relate to our cause.

- Getting to know **God** is the reason we read the Bible. God is the central focus of our devotion and conversation. ෬God becomes our haven whether we are at home or church, with family or in ministry. He becomes the refuge. ෬God's enemies are the same as were Jesus' enemies – those who say they know God but place restrictions on those who want to know Him.[36]

For years our family attended seminars, read books and attended workshops) in which godly children and teens (good fruit) were presented. For a mom like myself with no training (and no clue) on how to raise godly children, many things were new. Many times I fell into a dangerous trap of comparison when I saw how relatively low our standards were compared to new higher standards. God's good intention in this comparison was for me to look to Him and allow Him to speak to me about any need for personal change. Sometimes I did look to Him, and He would begin working on my heart, which usually brought about a change in some standards. Other times I looked to Him and sensed a peace that the new, higher standard I was seeing was not for me just yet.

Sometimes, though, I just tried to duplicate someone else's standard without a heart change. Adopting new standards looked easier than repentance and heart surgery anyway. *Besides*, I would reason, *look at the godly results (fruit) these families reap when they raise their standards.* It was a wrong conclusion, but those standards looked so attractive I would think, *We need to stop doing this, start doing that, dress like this, talk like that...*

This subtle turning away from a relationship toward a standard happened when I began desiring the fruit (godly children) more than the fruit-giver, Christ. This turned out to be an idol for me, and pushed me into legalism (trying to accomplish righteousness, bear godly fruit, by keeping standards and rules). That ended up producing death in the areas I tried to apply it. The harder I pushed, the more we experienced dead-ends such as the Husband-Digging-In-While-Children-Plummet-to-New-Lows Syndrome. This syndrome triggered the well-known Momzilla Meter which would begin pegging out to a tune called, "When Mama-Ain't-Happy...."

> The harder I pushed, the more we experienced dead-ends such as the Husband-Digging-In-While-Children-Plummet-to-New-Lows Syndrome.

When the fruit we seek to bear becomes more important to us than the pruning the Father wants to take us through (which often results in good fruit later, but at the time seems hard), we've allowed the fruit itself to become an idol. We then find standards and rules that will keep our idol in its place, rather than allowing those standards to become a question that we take

Parental Idols and Their Consequences

back to our Heavenly Father.

Lord, what do <u>You</u> want me to learn in this teaching (testimony, message, friend's life)?

I had to die, in a sense, to my vision (seeing my children's potential for Him), my hopes (that they follow Him with all their hearts), my needs (to be validated as a parent by myself or those around me such as parents or in-laws or other family members or close friends), and many other idols.

When I turned back to the Lord to serve Him knowing I would have to leave those good causes and follow Him alone, He was able to use me to help bring my family closer to Him! I was free from the idols that were keeping me from hearing His voice more clearly. I began to live like a true Christian before my family.

We parents can do all the right outward things to win and keep our children's and teens' hearts – have regular Bible study together, remove the television, teach them about God, serve in a ministry together and even choose a job where the father can be with his family all the time – and still lose them. Tragically, that is what's happening in many Christian families today. We're making the same mistake Israel did, letting something other than God capture our affection, blind our eyes and seize our children.

Young people (especially those who have high-achieving or highly-dedicated parents with high expectations) need to know (really know) that their parents' work, church, ministry or worthy cause is not more important to them than God, or than their relationship with them. They need to know their thoughts and feelings are more valuable. They need to be encouraged to express if they want to move on to something else, or begin their own career, or if they think the Lord is calling to them to, "Come follow Me."

A mom was once chatting with me about an organization her

family worked in that she absolutely loved. They were seeing people's lives change and she was thrilled to be making such a difference with her life. But when she turned to her daughter to ask some detail about the ministry, her teen apathetically shrugged her shoulders. The mom never missed a beat, excitedly returning to us with all of her attention. But, I saw her daughter look back at her mom in a way that said her dedication to that organization and to others had been trumping their relationship. That mom was so wrapped up in her cause that she lost sight of her daughter's needs.

> To love them in the same way we love ourselves is to treat them with the same respect, kindness and concern we'd want to receive if our roles were reversed, we in their shoes and they in ours.

Jesus said the greatest commandment was to love God with all our hearts, and our neighbor as ourselves. Our families are our closest neighbors! To love them in the same way we love ourselves is to treat them with the same respect, kindness and genuine concern that we'd want to receive if our roles were reversed, we in their shoes and they in ours. How blind we can become to the obvious when we cherish anything except the Lord. How wise it would have been for that mom to have shown more concern for the hurting "shrugger" who was right next to her than for those whom she had not yet met outside her home.

We need to be on our guard to keep the Lord in the center of our hearts. When He is in His rightful place, He helps us understand a little better, listen a little longer, speak a little softer, love a little deeper.

Years ago I was unhappy with Bill over some issues I didn't think he was handling very well, and my frustration was affecting the children. The issues were his responsibility, I

Parental Idols and Their Consequences

knew, but I couldn't escape the fact that I was the one who kept feeling the effects of them.

One particularly stressful day, one of those issues reappeared on the scene. It was a bad day for an issue to show up. I'd already been feeling overdrawn in my Kind-and-Loving-Mother account. For one thing, five of our seven children had been born in 6 ½ years. On top of that, they came with sinful hearts of their own. It had been going down hill from there. To survive, I'd been borrowing steadily from what resources I had left in the Model, Loving-Wife account. I wasn't feeling too kindly that day to the idea of digging into depleting stores of inner resources to spend on avoidable issues.

> Momzilla is the woman for whom the saying, "When Mamma ain't happy, ain't nobody happy" was coined.

As I was stewing over how I should properly respond to my problems (which, by the way, took a fraction of a second), I realized that something else had just appeared on the scene right along side this issue. It was Momzilla.

Momzilla is the woman for whom the saying, "When Mamma ain't happy, ain't nobody happy" was coined. There are also many other sayings coined in her name, but I can't repeat any of them in a book like this. She is the woman who can go from zero to ten in the flash of an issue. She is every husband's and child's nightmare.

And there, before my very eyes, I realized that I had transformed once again from loving wife and mother into Momzilla. With fangs. And with thoughts that raged and eyes that burned with fire.

It was times like those (and believe me, I've had my share of them) that God used to bring the state of my own heart (rather than the issue which had just gripped me by the throat) to my attention.

I stole away from the children to cry my eyes out, and to make my complaint known to God. After all, He was able to cause my husband to handle these issues differently, thus fixing my circumstances. But He never seemed in much of a hurry to do that, and I felt the strong need to bring that to His attention. Again.

Once I was alone I poured out my complaints to the Lord. It began with the issue that was choking me but that turned out to be only the beginning.

As long as I am going to complain to God, I reasoned, *I might as well let Him know everything that's bothering me.*

I was thinking in particular of my injustices in light of all of the sacrifices I'd been making for Him. When I was finished complaining, I waited. And waited some more. Then, I had a tiny thought. It went something like this.

Why don't you surrender your desire for happiness?

What a strange thought. Surrender my desire for personal happiness? I quickly reasoned that even missionaries in Africa, who give up houses and land and families and friends, got to have happiness when they were serving God. Why would *I* have to surrender personal happiness?

Suddenly, all of the things that I had already given to God came parading before my agitated mind. I'd given up a house with air-conditioning, central heat and modern conveniences so we could afford for me to be at home. I laid down my writing to have time for the children. I gave up new clothes and new appliances and benefits of every sort (which, by the way, I hadn't noticed Him asking many of my friends to do). In

Parental Idols and Their Consequences

addition, I couldn't see God putting any pressure on that Dig-in-His-Heels Husband of mine to change very much.

No, it always seemed that *I* was asked to change, to give more. And now I wasn't supposed to be happy, either? How could that be right? How could it be fair? I'd come to God asking for help, and the only help I received was the one thought that I'm supposed to make yet another sacrifice.

No, no, no! Why is it always me, me, me who has to change, change, change? And why do I always have to give, give, give?

My words may sound childish to you, but I was hurting at the time and my sacrifices were very real to me.

But where is a person to go when he finds himself in an argument with God? There are no higher courts, no places for appeal. I felt like Peter when Jesus told the disciples they'd have to eat His flesh and drink His blood if they wanted to remain His disciples. We can accept what He says, or we can leave. But where else could we go to hear words of eternal life? If we're committed to eternal life, we're stuck.

Feeling so stuck, I resigned myself to giving God all my desires for personal happiness. It was the greatest struggle I've had to date. I didn't know what my future would hold, but I was fairly sure that happiness wasn't going to be in it. I kneeled and told the Lord I was making an altar in my heart, and that I would place on it all my desires for personal happiness.

> Happiness is not a goal; it is a by-product.
>
> ELEANOR ROOSEVELT

An unexpected thing happened, though. Those desires wouldn't budge. You know when God is asking you for something and your mind says yes, but the fingers of your heart are clinging to it as though its next beat depended on it? That is where I was.

I then told the Lord I just couldn't let go of my desire for personal happiness, and suddenly remembered a prayer a friend taught me years ago based on the fact that He both *wills* and *works* in us His good pleasure.[37]

Lord, I'm not willing. But I want to be willing. Right now I give You permission to help me to be willing.

I waited, but again nothing happened. My heart was as stony and unyielding as before I prayed. I prayed again.

Lord, I can't budge this thing. But I give You permission, as the Great Physician, to cut it from me.

Again I waited, hoping my heart would at least soften toward the Lord, toward the issues that drove me to Him, toward my husband or myself. But, there all my issues and hurts remained, trapped behind a stony wall that wouldn't let them out.

And then another thought.

Why don't you climb onto the altar?

Climb onto the altar? That couldn't be right. I'm already a Christian, and I've already dedicated my life to the Lord. Besides, I've been to this invisible altar of sacrifice before and I know all I have to do is pull this thing from my heart and lay it there. That's the way it's always worked. I've never been asked to climb onto the altar before. No, that would be scary.

So, I waited. And then I remembered that surgery isn't

I felt like Peter, realizing there was no place else to go. Finally, resignation.

performed in a chair in the doctor's office, but on the operating table in the O.R. Suddenly, that little altar became an operating table in my mind, with me as the patient. That was much more risky and vulnerable than what I had expected.

Yuck! No way. I came here to ask for help, not surgery.

Again, I felt like Peter, realizing there was no place else to go. And then, finally, resignation.

Lord, I have nowhere else to go but to You. And if this is what You require, then I will place myself completely on the altar (though I'd like to remind You that I've done this before and I don't understand why You'd ask me to do it again). I'll climb up on that altar and give You permission to cut from me anything that You decide, even down to my desire for personal happiness.

Again I waited. But my spiritual feet were lead, my heart stone. I didn't have what it would take to even climb on the altar I'd made in my mind.

I'd never been to an altar like this, one in which I was asked to give something I could not, to surrender myself and would not. I felt terrible. If God weren't going to help me, what would I do? I welt like I was in a very bad pickle as the saying goes.

Feeling desperate, I meekly prayed one more time.

Lord, I can't do it. I guess I won't do it. But if You will, I give You permission to carry me to the altar.

And then a very sweet notion spread in my mind that God had been patiently waiting for just that prayer. I seemed to understand an important facet of Christianity in that moment.

1. God requires all of our heart.
2. We can't give it.
3. If we ask, He helps us give it.

I also saw that every sacrifice I'd ever made (and had paraded before him only moments before) had only been possible by His invisible help, and I could take no credit other than to say that I had received His help.

What a great insight!

The only problem was that even though I had this new understanding, I still didn't sense I was being carried to the altar. And when I thought about the issues that brought me there, my heart still felt cold.

And nothing else happened. I walked away with my cold heart and my hurt feelings, back into issues that I couldn't change, and that were still affecting me. Only now I had the knowledge that God was supposed to do the work in me and for some reason He didn't. And who knew when Momzilla would show up again? Needless to say, I was disappointed.

Sure enough, about two weeks later, the very same issue with my husband that had driven me to pray that day appeared and caught me unaware. My first response was the usual internal zero-to-ten feelings of the past. Only this time I stopped at, perhaps 7. And at that very moment I had the tiniest bit of grace and the tiniest thought.

This issue isn't my problem. It's Bill's. Lay it down.

Let me say that the grace I experienced in that millisecond of reaction time seemed like barely enough to stop me in my tracks. There wasn't a fraction more. But it was just enough to stave off a Momzilla-rerun, and even enough to accept any

Parental Idols and Their Consequences

possible effects the issue might have had on me.
    And that was all that happened. Until a few weeks later when the very same issue popped up again. I reacted again as in the past, but hit only about a, well, perhaps a 5. And there was that very small window of grace again.

This issue isn't mine. It's Bill's. Don't pick it up.

I had never had grace like that in the middle of a Momzilla attack before. Something was definitely changing. Not in my circumstances, but in me.
    And that is how it went. Over the next few years, chronic issues appeared, disappeared and reappeared. Grace appeared with them, usually not in abundance, but always just enough. When I yielded to grace, my Momzilla-meter kept going down; when I didn't, it went back up.
    As I saw the good fruit I was beginning to bear, I was heartened, which made it easier to respond again to grace. I was beginning to see buds of a good crop.
    And I was happier. The very pursuit I had been asked to give up had come into my heart in fuller measure.
    Though I didn't realize it at the time, much of my outlook and many of my decisions had been wrapped up in a pursuit of my own personal happiness rather than a pursuit of God. Becoming a Christian meant I wouldn't go to hell, and that would make me happy. Raising godly children, getting rid of issues, changing unpleasant circumstances, all would keep me happy, happy, happy. When my deepest motivations were exposed, they all revolved around my own personal happiness.
    Looking back, I wonder if I would have somehow bled to death if God had cut that idol from me on the day I asked. It had been fed for so long that it had grown quite large and wrapped its tendrils around and around my hear, mind and soul. Or

perhaps I just lacked the faith for Him to do it in one day. At any rate, I think what I went through over those years was a sort of "spiritual chemotherapy." Little by little, issue-by-issue, my cancerous idol of personal happiness grew smaller as it was zapped by the Holy Spirit as I yielded to His grace. And happiness, now removed from the center of my heart, was free to come and go as it should. What a difference this has made in my relationships with my husband, children and others.

> As long as we're seeking God there will be new areas of our hearts His love will want to expose and conquer.

I wish I could say I am completely idol-free. I *can* say that by His grace I am staying in remission on certain issues. I think as long as we're seeking God there will be new areas of our hearts His love will want to expose and conquer.

CONCLUSION

If you recognize idols in your own heart, it is so easy to get help. We ask. If we ask, God answers. We won't always like what He says, but He does answer. And if we do whatever He says, He will keep answering us when we ask again.

I have found it helpful to pray very simple prayers like this:

> Dear Father, I see I've let You slip from the center of my heart, and that other things have taken Your place. Some are good things, but they've been edging out my desire for You. Will You please forgive me? Will You do whatever it takes to remove them from the center of my heart, so that You can have Your rightful place? And please give abundant grace to those I've hurt in my blindness, and show me what You want me to say to

Parental Idols and Their Consequences

them or do for them. I ask for grace, help and mercy through Jesus. Amen.

Final note to this Chapter: It's late at night and I just (finally) finished this chapter. I don't want to think or type anymore. But as I slide my head down on the pillow (I'm typing on a laptop in bed), I flip open to the following words from today's entry for in the devotional, *My Utmost for His Highest* by Oswald Chambers:

When Paul received his sight, he received spiritually an insight into the Person of Jesus Christ, and the whole of his subsequent life and preaching was nothing but Jesus Christ – I determined not to know among you, save Jesus Christ, and Him crucified. Never allow anything to deflect you from insight into Jesus Christ. It is the test of whether you are spiritual or not. To be unspiritual means that other things have a growing fascination for you.

Well written. May we all come to the place where we desire to know Jesus more than we want anything else.

CHAPTER FIVE:

Bringing the Weak to Maturity ~ Helping Our Children to Hear the Lord's Voice

All that every came before Me are thieves and robbers, but the sheep did not hear them. John 10:8

*My sheep hear My voice, and I know them, and they follow Me.
John 10:27*

"What do you and Dad want me to work on this summer?"

It was the spring of 1996 when our oldest son, Jonathan, then fifteen, walked into the kitchen and mentioned that we still hadn't given him any direction for the summer. I looked up and thought to myself, "Wow. Life with our oldest is finally good." Only five years before, he and I'd been standing in that same kitchen arguing nose-to-nose about what I wanted him to do for the next *hour*.

It was in those years of crying out to the Lord and learning to hear and obey His voice of correction that I received help in gaining our son's heart back. Then, when he was about thirteen, we asked him to begin praying about what he thought the Lord might want him to do as an adult. He came back a few months later and said he thought he was supposed to go into law.

Up until that time, we'd been making steady progress at winning his heart. It felt so nice to be able to say to him, "Go and do thus," and see it done, and done well. His right attitudes and obedience showed us we were making progress. He was now always obediently waiting for our direction. Everything was finally feeling safe and comfortable.

So why in that moment did I risk all that comfort by saying, "Honey, why don't you pray and see what you think the Lord wants you to do, and let us know if you think He's giving you direction?"

> They that can give up essential liberty to purchase a little temporary safety deserve neither liberty nor safety.
>
> Benjamin Franklin

Though it seemed like a casual suggestion to me, given by a busy mom trying to get dinner on the table with a baby on her hip and a preschooler at her ankle, Jon confided to us years later that it was one of the scariest things I'd ever said to him. Bill and I now know it was because the Lord directed my words.

Here's why it was so scary. For Jon's part, life had gotten much easier once he committed to the Lord that he would obey his parents. His conscience was clearer, his motivations right, and he had been sailing on "easy street." That day his mom complicated his life by suddenly *not* giving him direction when he asked for it. He likened it to me walking him to a cliff and casually saying, "Sweetheart, why don't you jump off and see if the Lord teaches you to fly today?"

He didn't want to learn to fly; he liked the safe, comfortable nest of obedience to parents where everything was always lined up for him. His life had been limited to receiving and obeying direction, and he wasn't comfortable with the idea of trying to figure out what that direction was supposed to be. He wondered whether God would answer him if he asked for direction for the summer. He was born again, and felt confident he had heard God's direction for his career, but smaller, more every day direction seemed risky. What if he got the answer wrong or misheard the Lord's voice? What if this God that seemed to speak to his parents didn't speak to him?

Bringing the Weak to Maturity

"Hearing God's voice" simply means being able to sense God's direction in our spirit. Some call it getting a "green light" (a 'yes') or a "red light" (a 'no') in our hearts in answer to prayer. Or a brand new thought comes to mind and we recognize it is the Holy Spirit bringing that thought.

> For all who are being led by the Spirit of God, these are sons of God.
>
> ROMANS 8:14

We have to be "born again"[38] to sense the Spirit's direction within our spirit. If we don't learn to discern His voice, we'll make the mistake of allowing circumstances, feelings, philosophy, our own wisdom or other people determine direction for our lives. And if we use the Bible *alone* for direction, we run the risk of ending up like the Pharisees who searched the Scriptures but never recognized or came to Jesus.[39]

> The Spirit Himself testifies with our spirit that we are children of God...
>
> ROMANS 8:16

God's voice will never contradict the Bible, but it may be very different than what He speaks to others who know the Bible. We know by our own conscience, by the fruit (or lack of fruit) in our lives, by our own private thoughts and private lives whether or not we'd consider ourselves to be hearing and obeying God's voice. We know down inside, in the deepest part of our heart, where our integrity lies and where the Holy Spirit brings conviction. This truth is not to be confused with demonic possession or mental illness, where people hear literal voices in their heads and believe it is God or other beings telling them to do unscriptural, unlawful things and unspeakable things.

If we are hearing and responding to God's voice, we can help our children understand what that's like, and gently encourage them in the same direction. Gently pointing them as they mature to turn first to the Lord instead of us is an important shift in Christian parenting. We parents can seriously err by giving too much direction for too long. It's just easy to do. And if we mistakenly believe it's our God-given duty to completely control our children's reins all the way to (and sometimes through) adulthood, we can really make a mess of things.

> He who has ears to hear, let him hear.
>
> MATTHEW 11:15

Jon did begin to receive direction from the Lord that summer as he began to seek Him on his own. We concurred with him that it was what we thought he was supposed to do. In the years since that summer, however, he's had to obey what he believed was God's direction to Him when we didn't quite know, and at times when his Christian friends didn't concur.

Since that summer we've learned to ask each of our children to begin seeking the Lord for personal direction. The age to begin that is different with each child, but for our family it's been from about eleven to fifteen.

> To him the gatekeeper opens, and the sheep hear His voice; and He calls His own sheep by name and leads them out.
>
> JOHN 10:3

We ask questions like, "Have you ever thought of what kind of difference you could make in this world for the Lord?" or, "Have you thought about asking the Lord what direction He might be calling you in your future?" These types of questions have helped them to see themselves as a part of the larger picture. They begin to think about what role they can have in God's plan in this world.

We try to ask these questions gently and casually as we're walking alongside them, not confrontationally or enthusiastically as though we're expecting them to receive a lightning bolt answer by dinner time. If we sense a strong desire on our part to know what they're hearing, it probably means we still have personal needs we want filled through our children, instead of through the Lord. We need to ask the Lord to cut those unhealthy ties. If we put pressure on them for a calling *we* want or need or expect them to fulfill (take over the family business, join in the family's ministry, get a degree and be the success we were or weren't in our youth, etc.), we run the risk of making our voices in their heads louder than the Spirit's gentle voice in their spirit. I was nearly guilty of doing this with our second son.

JAMES

One day in 1999 I was running an errand with James, who was thirteen at the time, when the thought struck me that we hadn't asked him to begin praying about his future calling as we had Jonathan. James is very sweet by nature, but also very quiet.

> There are two types of education: one should teach us how to make a living, and the other how to live.
>
> John Adams

"Jamey, have you prayed about what the Lord might call you to do in your future?"

"No," came his simple, sweet reply.

"Well, do you have any idea yet what the Lord would call you to do with your life?"

"No Ma'am."

"Well," I responded, "this is the time of your life you'll want to be asking Him for direction."

"Okay." He smiled.

"Will you do that, Sweetheart?"

"Okay." He smiled again.

Jamey has always been compliant and content. I remember being worried when he was a baby because he rarely cried. One night I slipped into his room to make sure he was still breathing and found him smiling and playing with his fingers.

I pressed on, concerned that his contentment would make him complacent, and my wonderful advice wouldn't be heeded.

"If you could do something with your life to make a difference in this world for God, what do you think that might be?"

At that very moment we were driving past a dilapidated mobile home park. James looked over at it, then at me and said, "I'd fix up those trailers and rent them to people."

"Uh, yes, I see."

I sped up and dropped the subject, feeling fairly confident the Lord would guide him as he had Jon once he started seeking Him.

Several months later we were alone again and I remembered to check in with him. "Have you been asking the Lord for direction for your future, Jamey?"

"Yes. I think the Lord wants me to be a landlord. I think I could buy places like that mobile home park, fix them up into decent places for people to live, and rent them."

"I see."

I dropped the subject again.

In the meantime, James was continuing to struggle with academics in his middle school years. He was spending more time doing fix-it projects around the house or starting new

> He that is of God hears God's words. You cannot heart them because you are not of God.
>
> JOHN 8:47

> Everyone who is of the truth hears My voice.
>
> John 18:37

Bringing the Weak to Maturity

building projects (which he could do well and took pride in) and less time hitting the books (which he couldn't do well and which brought him frustration). This raised my concern level to near panic as he approached high school and I was sure he wouldn't be ready for college prep courses.

One day, worried that my son wouldn't be able to support himself or a family one day, I cried out to God. I just laid face-down on our bedroom floor and cried out to the Lord for help with James' academics and his future.

A day or two after I cried out to the Lord for James I "happened" to turn on a radio program that was explaining how right-brain dominant males struggled with academics in their early years, and then blossomed academically in their mid-teen years. Everything they described fit our Jamey to a tee.

I spent a week researching right-brain dominance, and Bill and I decided, along with James' evaluator's encouragement, that we should allow him to spend a year or two doing the things he was good at while giving his left brain time to kick in more fully. We'd allow him to progress "commensurate with his ability."

We read that right-brain dominant boys who were negatively labeled often lacked motivation to catch up when they were finally able to, so we presented Jamey's new school plan as a fun program, and he took to it with great enthusiasm. He enjoyed reading, so we shifted his academics to reading Christian biographies and autobiographies, classics and heroes of faith, four to five hours a day. He then had afternoons free to work on whatever projects he wanted to. He also took on maintaining an organization's website (a hands-on thing he

> Now character is higher than intellect.
>
> A great soul will be strong to live, as well as to think.
>
> Ralph Waldo Emerson

enjoyed learning to do), and traveled a bit with his dad learning how to cable networks.

About every three to six months, we'd try a little bit of algebra or grammar or spelling to see if he was ready for them, but he continued to struggle with them for two years.

This schedule was fun for James. But it was scary for me! Every once in a while I would have a panic-moment, "What if he never catches up? What if he never gets a good job? He's having way too much fun. Can this really be called school?"

Finally, just before he turned sixteen, we tried the algebra book one more time, and this time he was able to understand the concepts! He returned to a more academic track, and we started him back in grammar and spelling where he'd left off. He began progressing rapidly.

Even though I saw that my son had strong character, and was gifted in common sense, a sweet personality and incredible skills in hands-on projects, I was still battling a few private fears that he wouldn't find God's direction or that we weren't preparing him adequately. When I prayed about it and talked to Bill, I felt more confident we were on track; if I gave in to fears, I panicked.

Because I didn't fully let go of those fears, and I saw James catching up so steadily, I erred that first year back at the books and pushed academics a little too hard. James became a little discouraged, but pushed on.

Around the age of sixteen, three years after the first time I asked, I checked in with him again on that vision, "Sweetheart, have you prayed any more about your future calling?"

"Yes, I still think I'm supposed to be a landlord."

By this time, I was wondering if he *really* was seeking the Lord.

Landlord? Could landlording be a calling?

I was secretly hoping he'd come up with something a little

Bringing the Weak to Maturity

more, I don't know, spiritual.

One day, hoping to steer him in a more divine direction, I asked him, "Why would you want to be a landlord?" His answer was immediate, clear and sincere. "So, I can provide clean, decent places for people to live, not like those rundown mobile homes we saw. I could also have places for people to stay if they needed them, like a missionary or someone else in need."

At once I heard the same reasons Jon had given for choosing a law career four years earlier – to help people. I heard Jamey's reason because I asked. And for the first time, I listened.

We decided to tailor James' next year to equip him to go into business for himself. We put him through a 20-hour financial freedom video course (twice), got him to open checking and savings accounts, and because he had shown himself to be trustworthy on many other levels, we added him as a cosigner on our credit card so he could experience the cycle of budget, charge, and pay the balance in full. I will add here that once he became a working adult, he opted for paying cash for all his purchases rather than using credit cards, though his dad and I still use them.

The following year when he was seventeen he heard about a four-year plumbing apprenticeship program offered by our community college where a student could work for a plumbing company during the day and take classes at night. James was highly interested. He prayed about it and told us he thought the Lord wanted him to enroll. The work would pay well, fund property purchases, and give him a skill he'd need for his vocation. He interviewed the next day and was hired the following Monday. We "graduated" him from high school that day directly into his new job.

At this printing James graduated from the program and purchased his first property for cash. He believes he's supposed to go into business without going into debt. He works hard and the Lord continues to bless him. More importantly, he believes he's doing what God called him to do, and that gives him great satisfaction. I thank the Lord that despite my fears and preconceived ideas of what God's voice to him would have said, James is fulfilling his calling for his life. By asking him to seek the Lord's direction for himself, we began weaning him off of getting direction from us, and gently nudging him toward hearing God's voice.

Someone once told us not to ask our children, "What do you think you'll *want* to do when you grow up." They may *want* to make lots of money or be famous or powerful. Or they may want to do what they're naturally good at. It certainly looks like James is being called to do the very thing he loves.

But God has a plan for each of our children and sometimes He calls people to do things they *don't* want to do. It's our weakness being exchanged for His strength.

KATE

When Kate was thirteen and had given us her heart, we also asked her to begin praying about her future. Here's Kate's story.

> When my parents first asked me to pray about what the Lord might have me do when I grew up, I was surprised. It seemed like a long way off and I didn't know. I immediately thought of several things that sounded fun and exciting, but I kept returning to, "What does *God* want me to do?"
>
> A few months later I read something about nursing and thought, "Now that would be fun and exciting!" Helping people was something I always wanted to do, and I thought the emergency field would give me a perfect place for witnessing. I prayed about it, and the

more I did, the more confident I became that it was what God had for me.

However, a year later, when Kate was fourteen, she marched up to me somewhat distraught.

"Do you know what I just found out? Nurses have to give shots! And I have a huge fear of needles! And they have to change bedpans. And I don't think I could do bedpans. I must have misheard the Lord!"

"Well, perhaps you did," I said. "But don't be discouraged. Just tell Him exactly what you told me, that you're not sure you heard Him, and you need to start from scratch. Ask Him to show you again. He's very patient."

A week or two later Kate returned and said, "Well, I prayed again, and this time I know I'm supposed to get a nursing degree."

"Great," I said. "It sounds like you're beginning to hear His voice to you."

The next year when Kate was fifteen we began to gear her studies toward nursing, beginning with biology. We also kept open the possibility that her direction might change.

Two months into biology she said passionately, "I hate biology! I mean, who would even care about all this stuff? Not only that, I don't understand it! I really don't think I have what it takes to be a nurse."

At this point, I didn't know what to think. Kate is our third child, and her older brothers seemed to slide into the direction they believed they were supposed to go without a whole lot of fanfare.

"Well, do you still think the Lord might be calling you to get a nursing degree?" I asked.

"I don't see how He could be," she replied. "I would never make it through nursing school."

I prayed for her, talked to Bill, and the only thing I could think to tell her was that whatever God called her to do, He'd give her the grace and ability to do whenever she needed to do it. But I also reminded her that she was young in the Lord, and that sometimes we mishear Him and can mistake our own strong feelings for His direction. This was all part of her learning-to-hear-His-voice process. So, again I directed her back to just telling the Lord what she told me, and asking Him to confirm whatever direction He had for her life.

Later that week she came back and said, "Well, I prayed about my future."

"And?"

"And this time I really know I'm supposed to get a nursing degree."

"Really? Well, it does sound like you're beginning to recognize His voice. I'm so glad! Now back to biology, Young Lady!"

She groaned. But she made a commitment to obey God, and to work hard on biology despite her distaste for it.

During this same time, Kate told her dad she thought she was supposed to go on a mission trip to Mexico with family friends. We had no money in the budget to send her, and she had none. Bill agreed to the trip on the condition that the Lord provide the funds. Kate began to think about a job, while also praying for provision.

The next weekend Kate and I were visiting a museum when a woman approached us. She owned a successful modeling agency and had been watching Kate. She offered to hire her immediately, with the likelihood of television commercials and modeling. The work would be fun, the money exceptional, and she reassured me that parents had final say on all contracts and could be present on all shoots. I told her we probably wouldn't call but thanked her for talking with us.

Bringing the Weak to Maturity

As we left, I was suddenly aware of a small battle stirring in me. I was aware that Kate needed more money than she had ever needed to fund a trip more spiritually-edifying than she had ever taken. Now a fast and fun way to make that money had just landed in her lap, without her seeking it. In addition, I'd taken modeling classes during high school and found them fun and educational. I would have enjoyed seeing her benefit from the same training in how to sit, walk and carry herself more gracefully, as along as it wasn't more sensually. Kate is also naturally tall and thin. *What*, I wondered, *if she could make an impact in the modeling industry without compromising her convictions?* Since we were being offered full veto power, I wondered if this totally unsought-for, out-of-the-blue offer was really God's provision and direction for her. Later that night I asked her what she thought.

"I've been thinking about it all afternoon," she said. "It is flattering. And tempting. And I think it would be fun. But," she sighed. "I've prayed about it and I don't think the Lord wants me to do something that would draw attention to my body. I just don't think it's what I'm supposed to do."

The next night Kate pulled up the agency's website and immediately recognized well-known celebrities who were this woman's clients. Eighteen months later Kate told us how much she'd struggled that night between what she was being offered from this world (doing what she wanted to do) and what she believed God was calling her to do (doing something she didn't want to do).

But God had more lessons on hearing His voice for all of us.

The next day a family friend called to ask if Kate could baby-sit full-time over the summer. Kate accepted. She was going to get to do something she truly loved: play with two little children all summer. And she'd have all the money needed for her mission trip. If that were the end of the story it would have been enough. But God had more lessons on hearing His voice for all of us.

My friend who asked Kate to baby-sit had her office in their home, so on many days she was able to spend time with Kate and the children. On one of those days, she noticed Kate plugging away at biology during the children's naps.

"Kate, how do you like that biology text?" she asked.

"I don't!" She said.

"Then, do you think it would be okay with your parents if I loaned you a different text and helped tutor you? I have a degree in chemical engineering, and I think I can help you understand it. I think you'd even enjoy it!"

With her new text and my friend's help, Kate did end up understanding and even enjoying biology.

"Mom and Dad, you'll never believe what I saw in a microscope today. God is awesome!"

Kate was very encouraged as she began to witness confirmations to her of God's voice to her.

But the following year, at age sixteen, she discovered she loved photography and enjoyed writing. In addition, she happened to meet two professional photojournalists in two different cities whose passion about their work was contagious. Kate immediately saw the potential for making a difference with her life while doing something she could really enjoy and do well. A few days later she came to chat.

"I'm just not sure about nursing anymore. I think I'd much rather write and learn photography."

"Have you prayed about it?" We asked.

"Well, no."

"Do you think the Lord may be redirecting you to write?"

"Could He? Would He?"

"Of course. But you need to know that He's directing you.

You don't want to jump ship because you want to do something else."

"But I don't understand! Why would God ask me to do something I don't want to do? Especially if I'd rather do something else?"

I smiled. "Welcome to Christianity 101, My Dear."

"Huh?"

"There will often be a cross between what you want to do and what you're called to do. We don't always want to take up our cross and follow Jesus, but we do it because He tells us to and because it's right. It's also good for us. All I can tell you is that God will reward you, and reward you abundantly, if you obey whatever His direction is to you."

She returned a few days later, assured once again after prayer that nursing was still the direction she was supposed to go. She passed up the photography class, and I was glad she had finally settled it.

Then Kate graduated from high school and attended a training program with Summit Ministries. It was very helpful and meaningful to her, and she returned full of new enthusiasm and vision. I think she was home about a millisecond when she asked if she could talk with me.

"Mom, I really don't want to go to nursing school."

By now I had a pretty good idea that she *was* being directed to go to nursing school. This was partly because of many confirmations, the Lord's hand of favor on her as she moved in that direction, and partly because each time she spent time alone for prayer, she came away with the same thing. I felt this was another test for her, but I knew that she had to work it out herself.

"Okay. Why do you think that?"

As she talked, it was easy to see that she'd been strongly affected by people who were making outstanding impacts in the world for Jesus. She wanted to be part of the action. And she *wanted* to do something she *wanted* to do.

I told her it was completely her decision, but that she should only make a vocation change if she felt that the Lord was leading her, and not simply because she wanted to. She said she'd pray about it again, but that she was pretty sure she'd missed the Lord with nursing.

The next day her acceptance to nursing school arrived in the mail, and within a few weeks she was feeling again like it was the right direction.

Kate passed her RN boards in 2007, and landed the job she was praying for at the E.R. at a trauma center in a nearby city. When I asked her one day over lunch if she believed it was Gods direction for her and whether she was enjoying her work, she enthusiastically said, "Yes." She had also forgotten most of her doubts until I reminded her of them! The Lord continues to confirm His direction to her and pour out His favor on her as she obeys Him.

If our teen has given us his heart, we want to begin asking him to pray about some of his decisions instead of asking him to automatically coming to us for direction. We know he'll make mistakes and stumble. We all do. There have been times in all our lives that we thought the Lord might be prompting us to do something, but we weren't sure. Sometimes we erred on the side of emotional enthusiasm or good intentions, sometimes on the side of caution.

> We know they will make mistakes and stumble. We all do.

How good and right it is for our children to begin discerning the Lord's voice for themselves while still under our roof, where mistakes have fewer consequences. How blessed is the son or daughter who is able to hear and obey the Lord's voice before they leave home.

Bringing the Weak to Maturity

DANIEL

By the time our fourth child, Daniel, turned thirteen he'd already decided he was going to be an Air Force pilot. Nothing could be more thrilling to him, and he was convinced that being a pilot would be his mission in life. Since he'd given us his heart and was developing self-government, we allowed him to join the Civil Air Patrol Cadet Program on the advice of friends who recommended it as good preparation for the Air Force.

All of our children are tall, and by the time Daniel was fifteen he was over 6'4", well on his way to catching up with James who was 6'6". It was at that time that we learned that the Air Force had a 6'5" height limit on pilots.

One night Daniel was alone with me in the van. Glancing over at him I began to wonder why God would shut the door to something he was calling Daniel to do. Then I had a thought.

I wonder if being a pilot is Daniel's calling, or simply what he wants to do?

I tried to remember when he first told us he wanted to be a pilot, and I couldn't remember if he'd ever told us he'd prayed about it.

"Uhm, Daniel," I started, "did Dad or I ever ask you to pray and ask the Lord about your calling, or to ask the Lord to give you direction for your future?"

"No ma'am."

"I see. Well, have you ever prayed about it?"

"No."

No?! He's already fifteen and we've never asked him to pray about his future? How could we have forgotten to ask him that?

This is Bill's fault – why he should have... No, no, it's my fault – I'm the one who he asks to chat with them about... No, no, wait... Alright, Lord, I yield my son and his future to you. Would You please forgive us for overlooking this part of his training, and presuming on his future? Would You direct him and speak to him?"

"Um, Honey?"
"Yes?"
"Dad and I usually ask you kids to begin praying about your future. I know you've wanted to be a pilot for a long time, but would you be willing to give that desire to God and tell Him that you want Him to direct you in whatever direction He has for you?"
"Sure."

Sure? That was easy...

"Well, we can pray right now if you like."
As I drove home Daniel prayed that God would show him whatever He wanted him to do with his life. About a month later he told us that his strong desire to be a pilot was slowly shrinking.

When we ask our teens to begin seeking the Lord about their future, it definitely helps to make it a casual request and leave all the intensity for true emergencies. If we pressure our children to hear the Lord, or pester them to find out what we think He's saying, they feel that pressure.

HEARING FOR THEMSELVES

We also have to expect that they may mishear the Lord a few times before they begin to discern His voice. Stephen was

Bringing the Weak to Maturity

fifteen before he received direction to go into missions, but Patrick was ten when he knew he was being called into missions.

Sometimes they'll hear the Shepherd when we don't. One summer Daniel and Stephen asked if they could attend a summer encampment (a sort of boot camp) with Civil Air Patrol. I wasn't comfortable with the idea and expressed my concerns to Bill. He told the boys not to plan on it, and they said okay. Weeks later, I saw a deadline reminder for encampment in my inbox and my heart softened. My worries seemed to disappear and Bill gave his okay.

When I told Daniel he could still attend if he wanted to, he beamed a huge grin and said he'd been secretly praying that God would change our minds. What amazed me even more was that when I told Stephen he could go, he said the same thing. But, neither of them knew the other had been praying for God to change our minds. They had prayed about it, and knew they were supposed to go, even though Bill and I didn't know.

When Kate told us at the age of fifteen that she felt the Lord was directing her to go on a missions trip to Mexico, the only picture that came to my mind was that of my only girl spending a week in what I presumed would be crime-ridden areas of a foreign country. I didn't like the idea. But I had to admit that neither Bill nor I had "red lights" when we prayed about it. We didn't have any "green lights" either. But, *she* was telling us that she was getting green lights. We let her go and that week positively impacted her life.

Neither of them knew the other had been praying for God to change our hearts.

If our children begin to sense a pull in a certain direction after they start to pray, and if we pray for them and don't sense a strong negative check in our spirit (as opposed to strong, negative fear), then we want to help them to accomplish their goals. That help is different for each child.

Jonathan believed at the age of thirteen that God had called him to get his law degree through a private Christian online law school that didn't require an undergraduate degree. When he turned seventeen, he found out that his SAT scores had netted him a full four-year scholarship to the state university. Unknown to us, this unforeseen scholarship presented a temptation for him. His dad and other family members had attended this same university, so throughout his childhood he had a desire to attend there one day. He was now faced with the choice of a free ride at the state university with national recognition, or full tuition at an unknown, non-accredited, unconventional, out-of-state law school. For someone who had spent his entire life trying to explain homeschooling to everyone outside our family, the university was beginning to look safe and comfortable and, well – "normal".

After he prayed about it he told us he was going to give up the state scholarship to take the less-familiar road he thought God had called him to walk. It was a very personal, very tough decision for him that he felt God was leading him to do. Bill told me privately he thought Jon should also get his undergraduate degree at the state university, but he didn't mention that to him. He felt that Jon needed to hear that on his own. We put the state scholarship on hold.

During his second year of law school, a family friend who is also a father-figure in Jon's life and a professor at this same university encouraged him to use his scholarship. Jon prayed about it again, and believed he now had direction from the Lord to use it. Jon graduated from both schools and believes they were both God's will for him. He felt he was supposed to receive the ethical training he needed through the Christian law school, but also learn about secular academia, which has helped

Bringing the Weak to Maturity

him to understand the agenda he's now facing in the world.

Even though Bill felt it was God's will for Jon to attend a state university, he felt Jon needed to discover that on his own. Part of the reason is because state universities are loaded with temptations and traps in socialization, coursework, philosophy and agenda. Easy access to drugs, sex and alcohol, along with provocative dress, self-indulgent lifestyles and a party atmosphere mean that our children had better have clear direction, strong character and be walking in a self-governing manner before stepping on campus. Jon's time on campus was a daily trial, and we don't think he'd have been as well prepared for it had he attended straight out of high school.

Once Jon felt state university was the right direction, we worked hard to get him on and off campus as quickly as possible by researching CLEP credits, online courses and reviewing his schedule to make sure he graduated with the bare minimum 120 required hours – and not one more.

Without clear direction we would have discouraged our children from attending a secular college. State colleges, Christian colleges, junior colleges, secular workplaces, Christian workplaces, even mission fields all carry their own sets of traps – some obvious, some subtle. Even being raised in a strong Christian family has traps.

> Don't assume that your child is born again just because he repeated a childhood prayer or because he's in a strong evangelical family.

Children easily pick up on what a "good Christian" looks like and can make external changes to please parents and friends. We know three strong Christian families who thought their teens had been born again and were surprised when they later came to Christ as teens. Don't assume that your child is born again just because he repeated a childhood prayer or because he's in a strong evangelical family. If your teen is born again, but you don't think he's learning to discern the Lord's voice yet, just ask the Lord to help you know if you're to help him, or just pray and wait.

It's important to help our teens learn to hear God's voice because they need to have His continuous direction and grace for whatever path they're to take. Our first five children have been directed at one time or another to a state university, a Christian college, early and conventional graduations, apprenticeship, non-traditional school, distance-learning, CLEP credits, as well as part-time and full-time work.

Our children will take different paths, but they need to know how to hear and obey the same Savior.

> *Today if you will hear His voice, do not harden your heart as in the provocation, and as in the day of temptation in the wilderness, when your fathers tempted Me, proved Me, and saw My work. Forty years long was I grieved with this generation, and said, "It is a people that do err in their heart, and they have not known My ways."*
>
> Hebrews 4:12-15

CHAPTER SIX:

Giving Them the Truth of God's Grace

A Christian Parent's Responsibility

Behold, I send you out as sheep in the midst
of wolves. Therefore be shrewd as serpents,
and innocent as doves. But beware of men!

Matthew 10:16-17a
Behold, I send you out as sheep in the midst
of wolves. Therefore be shrewd as serpents,
and innocent as doves. But beware of men!

Matthew 10:16-17a

Not only do our children need to learn to hear the Shepherd's voice before they leave our homes, but they need to know how to accurately handle the word of truth.[40] The church today is barraged with doctrines that swing both liberal and legalistic.

When Bill and I chat with other Christian parents around the state or nation, we notice that many of us have not had the benefit of a Christian upbringing. Some come from broken or dysfunctional homes, with few role models. Those who were raised in Christian homes often lacked healthy role models. Our generation seems a little bit like those sheep without a shepherd that made Jesus so sad. Or like the Israelites, who in a daring and courageous moment obeyed God and brought their families out of Egypt, but then spent forty years in the desert frustrated, complaining and wandering about. Our generation seems a little lost, directionless, in need of guidance. Perhaps that's why so many of us attend how-to seminars on basics such as Christian living and parenting.

Because many of us lack a good foundation and example, it's easy to embrace teachings that sound Scriptural, especially if they're taught by a beloved pastor or admired leader, embraced by people we love or who appear to be bearing fruit.

There are other reasons it can be tempting for us to accept a new doctrine without digging into the Scriptures to confirm it. It can feel unsafe or unsettling to differ with established teachers who say their views are Biblically-correct or the only Biblical view. We might also feel ill-equipped to differ with those who are in the ministry full-time or who have earned a degree in religious studies, since they have more training and time to study the Bible, while our own lives are filled to overflowing just earning a living and raising our children.

The Bible goes to great lengths, however, to assure those of us who are born-again that we are not only able to discern truth, but we are obligated to.[41] Jesus chose poor, uneducated men to enlighten with the simple truths of the Kingdom of God. We all need to be a little more like the Bereans[42] who searched the Scriptures daily to see if the new teachings they were hearing were true. Knowing how to search the Scriptures accurately is certainly a quality we want our children to possess before they leave our home.

We also need to be careful not to simply follow a man's teaching about Christ rather than Christ Himself. Paul warned the Corinthians not to identify themselves by saying, "I am of Paul," or "I of Apollos" or "I of Cephas," but rather to all be of Christ.

There are three simple ways we've shown our children to test a teaching to see if it is right doctrine:

- <u>Compare it to rest of Scripture</u>.[43] They need to see if a teaching continues to stand when it's put back into context and compared with the rest of Scripture, or whether it's being propped up by isolated Scriptures. Reading Scriptures apart from the rest of Scripture can give a totally different message than what was intended.
- <u>Check the witness of the Holy Spirit within us</u>.[44] Many of God's truths are spiritually discerned.[45] If

our children don't know how to discern truth, they'll be more apt to follow what feels or looks good, or do what others do. They need to know that a sense in their spirit that something is wrong, even if they don't know the exact why, is an important safeguard.

- <u>Inspect the fruit of the teaching.</u>[46] Fruit can't really be inspected unless we know the people who embrace the teaching, or go through a trial with them. It is very hard to judge fruit by a testimony from someone we've never met.

> Three ways to test a teaching:
> By the rest of Scripture.
> By the witness of the Holy Spirit within us.
> By its fruit.

False doctrine, rules of men, doctrines of men and teachings of men are some of the terms the Bible uses for teachings that don't line up with truth.[47] Our family has bumped into a few of them in the last twenty-plus years. We know they don't line up with truth because:

1) They don't hold up to the test of all of Scripture.
2) Our spirit doesn't bear witness with the Holy Spirit in us that they are truth.
3) Many people who are living by them are bearing bad fruit.

We live in a rebellious generation. Immorality and sin in the culture surround us. Jesus also came to a rebellious generation. Many Jews had turned away from following the Lord and didn't have the Scriptures in their hearts. They had allowed themselves to become absorbed into the culture, and then developed stony hearts and adopted many of the Roman ways. This was heartbreaking to Jesus, and He told His disciples that they had become so dull of hearing that He couldn't speak to them in anything but parables. Their spiritual receptivity and understanding had been limited. They were like sheep without a shepherd, wandering, directionless and lost. They had swung in the direction of the world.

But there was another group living in that rebellious generation, one that refused to conform to Roman influences. They witnessed the corruption of their generation, the compromises made by their less spiritually-minded contemporaries, and to the best of their ability, they resisted cultural changes, protected themselves and their families from outside influences, and made the Scriptures their highest priority. That group was the Pharisees. And in the most famous paradox in history, they murdered the very Redeemer they had spent their entire lives studying about.

It was to this group, those who knew the Scriptures better than anyone in town, that Jesus gave His strongest rebukes, calling them snakes and whitewashed tombs. It was of these experts in the Law that He said, "These people honor me with their lips, but their hearts are far from Me. They worship Me in vain. Their teachings are but rules taught by men."[48]

Those rebukes of the New Testament were directed at people who said they were speaking on God's behalf, but added their interpretation to God's word, embraced traditions or rules of men rather than of God, laid heavy burdens of teaching on men's shoulders that were hard for them to bear, or chose to live under law rather than grace.

We encourage our children to become very familiar the New Testament, to read it regularly and in context from cover to cover as a safeguard against error. It is the covenant into which they were born when they became born again, and it does an

Giving Them the Truth of God's Grace

excellent job describing what their relationship with God and others is supposed to look like. It is also passionately clear about the freedom that Christ purchased for them, and how impossible it is to please God if they try to live under the law. Having a solid understanding of the concepts of grace and faith, truths on which the New Testament are founded, are an incredible deterrent to falling prey to false teachings.

We'd like to share with you some of the discoveries we've made with our children as we searched the Scriptures with them to see if the things they were hearing were true.[49]

In Regard to Laws and Grace

There are two groups of people who allow rules (laws) to be placed on them in the New Testament: the weak[50] and the mature who want to reach the weak.[51] And there are two groups who *don't* allow rules (laws) to be placed on them: the lawless[52] and the mature.[53]

> All things are lawful for me, but all things aren't profitable. All things are lawful but I will not be mastered by anything…
>
> 1 Corinthians 10:23

When four different groups of people write, speak and preach about what each believes the true purpose of laws on a New Testament believer are (and what they believe they are supposed to look like), well, it can get pretty confusing.

The New Testament teaches that for the mature in Christ *all things are lawful.* An immature man clings to the security of rules and becomes susceptible to doctrines and commands of men rather than the law of God. A mature man limits himself *based on direction from the Lord.* An immature man easily mistakes his overly-sensitive conscious as true spiritual conviction, thus convincing himself that God has "convicted him" about things that are really only doctrines of men.

Doctrines of Men through Interpretations of Scripture

We also show our children how doctrines of men arise whenever someone's "interpretation of Scripture" (which come from verses taken out of context) is taught as a Biblical mandate (standard, principle, law or rule) for all believers, or "mature" or serious-minded believers.

We'd like to share with you just a few of the doctrines that are being taught to our young people today as "Biblical". We'll compare them to all of Scripture to see if they pass the test of truth and take a look at the fruit they are bearing.

> A less mature person easily mistakes his overly-sensitive conscious as true spiritual conviction, thus convincing himself that God has "convicted him" about things that are really only doctrines of men.

One teaches that God wants parents to remain in authority over children through adulthood. Parents are to shelter their children until the parents decide it is time to send them out into career, ministry or marriage. Single men and women living in the home or away from home must also receive their parents' permission and blessing for decisions on career, ministry or marriage, or they cannot receive God's blessing. In this doctrine, it is the parents' responsibility to hear from the Lord for their teen or adult child, and to transfer that direction to them. Some churches teach that pastors have these duties, and require members to gain their pastor's approval on life's decisions.

When we held these teachings up to the New Testament we saw them fall apart. We saw that 1 Corinthians 7 teaches that a single man or woman is free to please (answer to) the Lord, not

Giving Them the Truth of God's Grace

parents, and in John that there is no Scriptural support that one adult is supposed to hear the Shepherd's voice for another (unless it is as prophecy).

Here are some of the things we saw:

- Jesus did not speak first to the disciple's parents about their children or their calling.

- Jesus did not ask any of the disciples' parents' permission when He called them.

- The disciples were not "sent out" by their parents when Jesus called them.

- The disciples left their nets and their parents' homes to obey Jesus.

- Jesus never instructed anyone to ask their parents if they could follow Him.

- The angel Gabriel spoke to Mary, a very young teen (not to her parents, and not to her husband-to-be – both considered authorities in her life) when he brought her the news that she would be the mother of Jesus.

- God could have had Moses write "a man shall <u>be sent out</u> by his father and mother and cleave to his wife" if He had wanted us to understand that a man wasn't supposed to leave home until he was sent out by his parents. But Jesus, quoting Moses, said, "For this reason <u>a man will leave</u> his father and mother[54]

- Eli was a poor father-figure but helped Samuel recognize the Lord's voice. Samuel's first word from the Lord, while he was yet a minor, was a *rebuke* to his "father" Eli.

- The book of Proverbs is filled with parental advice about adult situations like adultery, prostitution, finances and marriage that show they are the child's decision to make alone, when the parent isn't there.[55]
- Jesus taught that children are to love God more than their parents, not love God through their parents.[56]
- Jesus told a man to leave his father to follow Him (he didn't tell his father to send the man to Him).[57]
- Jesus promised great rewards to those who leave father and mother for His sake.[58]
- If God intended for New Testament parents to send their children into ministry, it's reasonable to think that Jesus could have rephrased His call to say, "And everyone <u>who has been sent out</u> from father or mother, leaving houses or brothers or sisters or children or field for My sake will receive a hundred times as much and will inherit eternal life."

> A tree is known by its fruit.
> MATTHEW 12:33

In our culture, legally speaking, a child reaches adulthood at the age of eighteen. But Mary was probably thirteen or fourteen years old when God considered her adult enough to carry and deliver Jesus, marry Joseph, and begin raising the rest of her children. Mary certainly conducted herself as an adult. Perhaps that's why God considered her as one! Children mature into adulthood when they conduct themselves as responsible, self-governing adults.

We also had to look at these teachings in the light of what kind of fruit they are producing. We have seen many role models uplifted at seminars that promote these doctrines as those who are bearing good fruit, but we have met very few where this is the case. Instead, our hearts have broken with many friends and acquaintances who have damaged or lost complete fellowship with their teen and adult children by trying to control them for too long. We have heard from many more.

When we parents assume the role of hearing from the Lord for our children, we can miss it. We could either send them out too early where they face temptations and choices for which they have not been prepared, or hold onto them for too long, sheltering them as young adults from finding God's will in their lives. Parents may require children to fulfill the parents' vision (the children stay in our family ministry of take over the family business, etc.), or fulfill someone else's vision for them (a parent or grandparent or someone else for whom a parent has great respect or from whom they sense great pressure), or even fulfill a parent's own vision for their child (they force or emotionally compel their child to do what the parents believe God wants them to do).

We err if we usurp God's authority. God is the One who calls people, and He does so without consulting their parents.[59] If our children are born again, they're should begin hearing and obeying *God*.

Our son Jonathan, who is twenty-six at this printing, has witnessed the damage these kinds of teachings have produced in his own generation.

> I have seen some parents get so caught up in parenting that they completely miss the point. They are so obsessed with being great parents and protecting their children from the world that when God begins to whisper, "It's time for Me to begin replacing you in this child's life," they can't hear Him. They can't let go.

This response unnaturally extends "childhood."

It is easy to get so caught up in the process that you miss the goal. Keeping an adult in a child's role is unnatural and stunts the potential that God has for each person. It sets children up for failure. When will adult children learn to handle liberty?

The all-or-nothing transition of authority I have seen is like confiscating every penny a child earns from birth to age twenty-one and then handing him a credit card with an unlimited credit line. Unless he's an exceptional person, he's going to get into trouble.

Of course, all children will fail at something, but we should be willing to accept that. If we put ourselves in the place where God should be, we're stealing from God. This is a very serious sin.

If God is capable of speaking to a parent, then He is capable of speaking to an adult child. A parent is simply one who is temporarily placed in authority over God's children.

Doctrines of Men from Imitating Biblical Accounts Rather than Obeying New Testament Instruction

We also saw that some doctrines arise from Biblical accounts or patterns rather than Biblical instruction. We had to ask ourselves this question: "If this were an accurate way to teach doctrine, how would we know which accounts the Lord wanted us to imitate and which ones we should avoid?" Looking strictly at the New Testament, and based on "Biblical accounts: we could say that "Biblically speaking" we have a good argument for our daughters to marry around the age of thirteen, as Mary probably did. Or that because James and John immediately left their nets to follow Jesus that a New Testament

Giving Them the Truth of God's Grace

principle was established that all believers should *immediately* leave their homes, families and businesses the moment they are called. Or that because the gospels didn't record the disciples telling their fathers goodbye that it was not "scriptural" to do so.

For example, what should we do with the following "Biblical accounts" relating to marriage?

- Abraham slept with his wife's maid.
- Abraham slept with concubines after Sarah's death.
- Abraham's servant prayed that God would show him the right woman for Isaac by a sign. The sign was having her ask a certain question. His prayer was answered.
- Abraham sent a ring to be put in Rebecca's nose for Isaac.
- Jacob served seven years in trade for his wife.
- Jacob took two wives, fathering children with both.
- Jacob slept with concubines, fathering children with them. Those children became part of the twelve tribes of Israel.
- Isaac and Rebecca consummated their marriage without a wedding ceremony.
- The sons of Benjamin chose wives from the women who danced.
- Judah told his widowed daughter-in-law to wait until his other son grew up to marry him.
- Caleb gave his daughter in marriage as a prize to the man who captured a city for him.

- Ruth followed her mother-in-law's counsel and snuck into Boaz' bed to lie at his feet when he was drunk.
- David, a man after God's heart, paid for his wife with 100 foreskins.
- David married several women.
- David slept with many concubines.
- God told Hosea to marry a prostitute.
- Gideon married many women.
- Gideon slept with concubines.

These accounts aren't about ungodly people, but the patriarchs of Judaism. God's chosen people. And there is no indication of God's displeasure with them for their actions!

God Himself tells Israel in a metaphor that when He found her filthy in her sins, He cleaned her up and *put a ring in her nose* and earrings in her ears.[60] He said this as a compliment If we're going to use the Old Testament for rules to live by, we'd have stronger support for multiple wives and physical signs based on God's own words than for parents choosing their children's spouses based on examples. And nose rings for our daughters would be "Biblical."

> But if you are led by the Spirit, you are not under the Law.
> GALATIANS 5:18

It's clear that Old Testament examples weren't designed to be the textbook for New Testament relationships. Using the Old Testament in this way is dangerous, especially since the New Testament instructs us to view the Old Testament as an *example* so that we learn not to 1) crave evil things, 2) be idolaters, 3) act immorally, 4) try the

Giving Them the Truth of God's Grace

Lord or 5) grumble.[61]

Two other purposes for the Old Testament is that it 6) gives wisdom that leads to salvation through faith in Christ[62] and all Scripture is to 7) equip us for every good work.[63]

The Apostle Paul often quoted the Old Testament, but only to drive home the New Testament truths of faith and grace in Christ Jesus. He *rebuked* the Jews for telling Gentiles to keep the Old Testament command of circumcision. I wonder what he would have written to those who turn Old Testament examples and patterns into New Testament rules and laws.

The books of Romans and Galatians have been very helpful to us in understanding how valuable our freedom is Christ is and how dangerous it is to return to Old Testament customs.

Turning to Old Testament Standards Rather than New Testament Instruction

We also found that doctrines of man can come from turning to Old Testament standards rather than New Testament instruction. Some of those standards being taught to parents and young people are in the area of relationships.

Courtship is meant to be a step between friendship and engagement. Friendship—Courtship—Engagement—Marriage. It means more-than-friend-and-considering-engagement.

Dating means spending time alone with someone who is more than a friend, or who we want to become more than a friend, which may lead to engagement and marriage.

Friendship—Dating—Engagement—Marriage.

Dating carries a certain amount of expectations and temptations, so let us be clear that we have asked our teens not to date. We'd like them to keep their focus on their studies and other preparations for their futures while they have the time to be single-focused. We would also like for them to be spared the frustration of close emotional attachments that can't be fulfilled until they're old enough to marry. Since the teen years are marked by huge bursts of hormones coupled with not-fully developed emotional maturity, it doesn't seem fair for us to put our teens into that much temptation.

However, dating in itself isn't evil; dating simply tests maturity and self-control. When Jon was in his twenties and just about through college, he took a very special young lady out on a few dates. She was the first and only girl he'd ever dated, and he didn't ask her out until he was fairly sure she was the one he'd marry. They were not in sin to date.

There are certain teachings, however, that are laying an incredible amount of weights on Christian young people's shoulders in regard to relationships, much more than they were meant to bear. These weights are taught as being Scriptural, Biblical, God's will, or God's best.

Below are some doctrines our family has encountered.

- It is a father's Biblical duty to help find his children's spouses.

- A young man must ask his father's counsel and permission before expressing any interest in a young lady.

- If his father approves of both the girl and the timing, the young man must ask permission from the girl's father to see his daughter.

- At this point, the girl's father places any stipulations he thinks are necessary on the young man before he grants permission for him to see his daughter.

- The young man is not allowed to discuss his feelings or talk of marriage with the girl unless he

Giving Them the Truth of God's Grace

has been granted his father's permission to ask for her father's permission to discuss it with her.
- Unless both sets of parents (and sometimes all sets of step-parents) give their blessing, the couple cannot marry.

We understand the strong pull toward conservative standards like these. It is a natural reactionary swing away from the license we see in the world (and sometimes in the church). But Abraham himself would have been rejected with standards as strict as these! How many fathers today would approve of a man sending *someone else* to pick out a wife for his son as Abraham did? How many would let a stranger give his daughter expensive jewelry *on the day he meets her* as his servant did? *Before* meeting her family? And in the name of a man whom they hadn't seen in years, and whose son they hadn't met? And whose character they hadn't witnessed?[64]

> For there is one Mediator between God and man, the Man Christ Jesus.
>
> 1 TIMOTHY 2:5

We believe God wants us to teach our children to emulate Abraham and the other patriarchs in regard to their *faith*, not their *culture* or *traditions*.

Placing anyone, parent or pastor, between a maturing teen or an adult child and their Heavenly Father to hear His voice for them or to make personal decisions for them is actually placing a mediator between God and man.[65] But there is only supposed to be one Mediator between God and man – the Man Christ Jesus.

We once heard someone teach that Jesus' relationship to His Heavenly Father was the example of what our children's attitudes should be to their own earthly fathers. As Jesus said to His Father, "Not My will, but Yours be done," so our children are supposed to say to their father, "Not my will, but yours be done." We believe that a more correct view would be that Jesus, our older Brother, shows us by example how all of God's children are to relate to God. Jesus' relationship to His Heavenly Father should be compared to our relationship with our Heavenly Father, or to our children's relationship with their Heavenly Father – not to the earthly father. God's will, not ours no matter the cost – not an earthly father's will no matter the cost.

We also see some teachings that pull daughters today in two different directions. One is the view that a four-year college degree and/or career is the minimum for any Christian woman today. We believe that the "college and/or career is mandatory" view diminishes the extremely important and fulfilling role of wife and mother in our daughters' eyes, In addition, if parents view education as highly important, they will be tempted to let their teens' education overshadow their spiritual development. We see this with many teens who are allowed to take advantage of high school dual-enrollment and college classes before they're emotionally or spiritually mature enough to handle the environment or material. And many are stumbling and falling.

The opposite view teaches that marriage, family and home are the only future, or the only worthy future, for which a young woman should prepare.

We believe that our daughters as well as our sons need to learn to hear the Lord's voice of direction for them. Some of our daughters will certainly sense the Lord's direction to bypass college or career to move directly into the role of godly wife and mother. They may want to devote their teen and young adult years to preparation for that calling. If they sense that is God's direction for them, they should have a certain sense of confidence that they'll meet the right person when it's time, rather than a nagging fear that they may never marry, or a sense of duty or obligation that they must.

If, however, a daughter views marriage as a goal, or a means of escape, or a dream in which she expects to live happily ever after, she'll never be happy in marriage. Neither will her husband! We want our daughters to have a Scriptural view of marriage, not whatever current teaching that might be making its rounds in the body of Christ. The Scriptural view of marriage is that it is a really good thing, but it definitely brings its own set of troubles.

> Parents who yield to a worldly line of thinking rob their daughters of future fulfillment and joy by diminishing the role of wife and mother in their eyes.

If you marry, you have not sinned; and if a virgin marry, she has not sinned. Nevertheless such shall have trouble in the flesh: and I want to spare you.[66]

However, many young ladies are being discouraged from or forbidden to attend college or take any higher learning courses that aren't related to home, family or the development of a home-business. Under this teaching, girls in their teens and twenties feel like they've been delegated to second class in the Kingdom of God as they wait for father or pastor, and then future husband, to hear from God on their behalf. They are sometimes provoked enough to marry early or leave home and cut family ties altogether.

The truth, of course, is that God wants daughters to hear and obey His voice just as He wants sons to hear and obey His voice.

My sheep hear My voice, and I know them, and they follow Me.[67]

We encouraged all of our teens, both our sons and daughter, to prayerfully consider whether the Lord wanted them to attend college or not. Our first four (now adult) children have been directed by the Lord at one time or another to attend a state university, a community college, an online Christian college, an online secular high school and college, an apprenticeship program, early and conventional graduations, CLEP credits and an internship as well as hold down part-time and full-time jobs. Our next two children (who are still teens at this printing) think they are being called to the mission field, but both believe the Lord may also allow them to bypass seminary. Many different children, many different directions, one Lord leading them.

We also took a look at a New Testament passage that has been used to support the idea that a father has Biblical authority to control his daughter's future. 1 Corinthians 7:36-38 says, "But if any man thinks that he is acting unbecomingly toward his virgin daughter, if she should be of full age, and if it must be so, let him do what he wishes, he does not sin; let her marry."

We'd like to share with you three things we learned about that verse when we looked up the meanings of the words:

1. "Let them marry" has been translated from the word "gameo." The first three meanings of "gameo" are actions a person takes *in regard to one's self.* A more correct translation would be: "Let <u>them</u> get married."
2. "Virgin" has been translated from the word "parthenos" which also means "<u>virginity</u>."
3. The word "daughter" *never* appeared in the Greek. Translators *added* it.

The Darby Translation, which stays with the original Greek (and without adding any extra words to the text) translates that verse:

But he who stands firm in his heart, having no need, but has authority over his own will, and has judged this in his heart to keep his own <u>virginity</u>, he does well. So that <u>he that marries</u> himself does well, and <u>he that does not marry</u> does better.[68]

This closer-to-the-original translation is consistent with the rest of the New Testament's teaching on singleness and marriage. As a matter of fact, we saw that Paul addresses single daughters in the same chapter.

Now concerning virgins I have no command of the Lord…[69]

Singleness is obviously the stage between childhood and marriage, and the Bible describes it as *freedom* from both concern and family responsibility.

But I want you to be free from concern. One who is unmarried is (free to be) concerned about the things of the Lord…. And the woman who is unmarried, and the virgin, is (free to be) concerned about the things of the Lord that she may be holy both in body and spirit…But one who is married is concerned about the things of the world, how she may please her husband…[70]

We saw that there are two binding family relationships in the New Testament: parent and child, and husband and wife.[71] Singles are not bound with duties and obligations in a human institution, which frees them to more fully serve the Lord.

Some of our daughters will certainly be called to remain single. Annie Armstrong, Corrie ten Boom, Amy Carmichael and Lottie Moon were just a few of the many women who heard and obeyed God's voice to them and remained single. These women weren't dependent on their parents' permission or church leaders' approval to fulfill their extremely fulfilling callings, nor did they receive their callings through their parents or church leaders. These women saw themselves correctly as bound by and dependent on God's word and the Shepherd's voice as He led them. They lived extraordinary, rewarding and life-changing lives. They traveled the world, created and ran organizations, met and worked with world leaders, faced opposition, overcame fears and led many to Christ. Many received a higher education in obedience to the Lord. Until she marries, a single daughter remains free to be concerned with the things of the Lord.

Most daughters, however, will marry. As we think about our own daughter preparing for marriage one day, we see more teachings that can bind her, teachings too numerous for us to review. A few of these teachings say that a Christian wife should never:

- work outside the home.
- help support her husband financially.
- have her own vision or calling from the Lord apart from her husband's.

It is true that once she decides to marry, a woman's perspective shifts to concerns for the needs of her husband, new home and family.

But one who is married is concerned about the things of the world, how she may please her husband.[72]

It is also important to note that a man must shift his focus to pleasing his wife when he marries.

But one who is married is concerned about the things of the world, how he may please his wife, and his interests are divided.[73]

On the topic of being a worker at home, Paul tells Titus to have older women *encourage* younger women to be workers at home.

So that they may encourage the young women to love their husbands, to love their children, to be sensible, pure, workers at home, kind, being subject to their own husbands, so that the word of God will not be dishonored.[74]

Paul doesn't write that wives *must* work at home, or that they should work at home to the exclusion of working outside the home. He simply asks Titus to *encourage* young women to be workers at home. Holman's Christian Standard Bible translates it to mean "encourage them to be…good homemakers."

Paul also writes to Timothy about younger women.

Therefore, I want younger widows to get married, bear children, keep house, and give the enemy no occasion for reproach.[75]

Putting this verse back into context, we found that Paul had been addressing a problem he had been seeing with younger widows.

At the same time they also learn to be idle as they go around from house to house, and not merely idle, but also gossips and busybodies, talking about things not proper to mention.[76]

Those widows had some choices to make with their new free time. One choice could be to serve the Lord with a whole heart, which is what Anna did when she lost her husband after seven

Children of Character II

years of marriage and then spent the rest of her life serving the Lord in the temple.[77] They could have used their time to do good and serve the poor like Tabitha's example.[78] Or they could marry again. But these new singles were wasting their time and others' by gossiping and being idle, so Paul gave them another option to keep them busy: get married again and have children! Every mother knows how much more serious we become about our own spiritual life once we find ourselves married with children who are dependent on us for wise instruction And how little time we have left for gossip!

When put back into context, it appears that Paul was very likely saying something like: *Timothy, these younger widows obviously need something to do! If they're not going to use their freedom to please the Lord now that they're single again – well, then, tell them to get married and keep house. Then, they'll be busy enough! They won't any have time to be idle, or to spend time chatting at their friend's houses, or criticizing and judging other people.*

Some churches even have doctrines of man that teach that women cannot wear any jewelry or fine clothing based on two verses.

> ...whose adorning let it not be that outward adorning of plaiting the hair, and of wearing of gold, or of putting on of apparel...[79]

> In like manner also, that women adorn themselves in modest apparel, with shamefacedness and sobriety, not with braided hair, or gold, or pearls, or costly array...[80]

If we teach our children to look for dos and don'ts and cling

Giving Them the Truth of God's Grace

to rules, they could conclude from these two verses that God would want a young lady to refuse a pearl necklace or a gold ring or a beautiful dress that a father or husband gives as a gift from the heart. But Paul was using those examples to *compare* outer adornment to inner beauty. The message is that it is the heart attitude and loving actions that make a woman truly beautiful, and that women shouldn't *seek* beauty through outer adornment:

But let it be the hidden man of the heart, in that which is not corruptible, even the ornament of a meek and quiet spirit, which is in the sight of God of great price.[81]

…but (which becomes women professing godliness) with good works.[82]

We also looked at the most famous passage about wives of all, Proverbs 31, the excellent wife. We found it insightful to see how much freedom this Old Testament wife had in her marriage. Here are some excerpts from Proverbs 31.

According to Scripture an *excellent* wife 1) brings in her own income, 2) purchases real estate, 3) has her own clothing line and 4) markets it and 5) has her own wine label. The Scriptures *praise* her for those pursuits, particularly in the light of bringing her husband material gain! She also 6) takes the time to keep herself in good physical shape. And 7) she wore fine, expensive clothing. Whether it was with her husband's resources or her own income, 8) she hired others to take care of some or all of her household duties while 9) she was busy doing things that brought her delight and profit.

Children of Character II

The heart of her husband trusts in her, and he will have no lack of gain.
9) She works with her hands in delight.
She gives food to her household and portions to 8) her maidens.
2) She considers a field and buys it.
1) From her earnings 5) she plants a vineyard.
6) She girds herself with strength and makes her arms strong.
All her household are clothed with scarlet.
She makes coverings for herself.
7) Her clothing is fine linen and purple.
3) She makes linen garments and 4) sells them, and supplies belts to the tradesmen.
She extends her hand to the needy.
She opens her mouth in wisdom and the teaching of kindness is on her tongue.
She looks well to the ways of her household, and does not eat the bread of idleness.
A woman who fears the Lord, she shall be praised.

> The heart of her husband trusts in her.
> PROVERBS 31

Still, the most important points about this woman, and the real message of Proverbs 31, is that her *motivation* was right (she fears the Lord), she was kind (the teaching of kindness is on her lips), and she had won her husband's heart (the heart of her husband trusts in her). With her priorities right, she got to enjoy staying busy doing those things that were delightful to her (she works with her hands in delight), and worthy (she extends her hand to the needy). And she didn't allow those projects, as fun or rewarding as they were, to crowd out her home life (she looks well to the ways of her household). The Apostle Paul would have been pleased.

We let our sons and daughters know that God may direct some women to continue in their calling after marriage, even though they received that calling when they were single. Elisabeth Elliot is only one example of a wife who continued in her call to the mission field after her marriage, allowing the Lord to meld her calling with his as they worked side-by-side on the field until his death. Her calling complemented his.

A wife might even receive direction from the Lord to financially support her husband during an illness or while he finishes his education, or as her ministry to him as his "helpmeet." If the Lord directs her to do so and her husband concurs, the Lord will provide all the grace she needs to balance work and home. She'll want to make sure of her motivation, though, so that she doesn't work simply from personal ambition, because she's driven by fears about finances, because it's easier to work than deal with home issues, against her husband's advice or in disobedience to God's will for her. Being a helper to her husband (liberty) isn't the same as doing her own will (license).

> We want our daughters to have a Scriptural view of marriage, not whatever contemporary view is passing through the world – or the church – at this moment in history.

What if the calling a woman receives while she is single doesn't complement her new husband's? If her husband recognizes that she was a source of blessing to others before they married, it may give him great satisfaction to see her continue. In this way, a wife would please her husband while continuing in her calling.

An important question we want a daughter to ask herself before marriage is if she would be willing to subordinate the calling she received as a single to the new needs she'll encounter in marriage, especially when she has children. She may not need to; her calling may fit very well around her new duties.

But it is terribly important that she be willing. If she's very satisfied in her labors as a single and doesn't want to give them up, she'll find it nearly impossible to shift from pleasing the Lord freely as a single to learning to live intimately with, and please, a husband, and then invest in nurturing and training her children.

We want our daughter to have a *Scriptural* view of marriage, not whatever contemporary view is passing through the world – or the church – at this moment in history.

A Few Thoughts from Bill

We see two basic ways parents are training their children in Christian homes. One way is to train the child that the parent is the ultimate authority in their life until they move out to marry and start their own family. For a daughter, this means that parents transfer that position of authority to her husband. For the son, it means they will transfer it to God when he starts his own family. In this scenario, a daughter is never in a position to hear and be responsible to God directly. Sons are never expected to obey God directly (only to "obey their parents in the Lord") until they have their own families. This is very much like expecting a child to know how to drive a car without the benefit of any driver training.

> A young person eventually grows weary of being controlled...

I pity the wife or children who have to stay under the authority of a young man whose first real test of obeying God (and being in authority himself) is while he is trying to start his new family. We have watched a number of young people sent out from the authority of parents into marriage or career make extremely poor financial and life decisions. A young man may "get it" eventually, but it is going to be hard on those around him while he learns. For a daughter, it's like being forced to ride in the car with someone who is learning to drive, but who has only watched other people drive, and never had any real behind-the-wheel training. He will probably learn to drive eventually, but it is going to be very bumpy and unpleasant for everyone involved.

Parents who train their children this way don't see the need for a daughter to "get a driver's license" (hear from God herself) since her husband is going to be the one driving (hearing from God for both of them). Because of this, they sometimes go to great lengths to guarantee that the young man understands the laws of the road before they give her permission to ride in his car.

If the parents believe they still have full authority over their children's decisions, but their children believe it's time they be allowed to drive, there will obviously be strain in the relationship. What we're seeing in these families is that a child eventually grows weary of being controlled and comes to the conclusion, usually through frustration, but sometimes through Scripture, prayer or counsel, that he is old enough to move from a position of being under direct control. He believes he is capable of weighing his parents' counsel (giving honor), his own understanding of the situation, and (hopefully) his understanding of God's will to make his own decision. He may see it as a matter of trust between him and his parents. He may see his parents' opposition to what he believes as being "too controlling." Stress can be controlled until the first time the child feels strongly enough about a parental decision to object. If they take control of the wheel on their own, but have been given no training on how to drive themselves, they will probably make some bad judgments. They might have an accident. They might even bump into us on their way out, and hurt us a great deal. At this stage, unless they believe that the parents aren't going to jerk the steering wheel out of their hands and take full control of their direction again, they're probably going to steer clear of them. They would rather try to trust their own judgment or God.

We have nearly twenty years to teach our beliefs to our children. If they arrive at adulthood not agreeing with us, there is a foundational problem – either with our teaching or their acceptance. The actual crisis at-hand is not the real problem; it's only the catalyst that has brought the real problem to light. That problem usually won't get fixed during the crisis that revealed it.

The second way to train children is for parents to work themselves out of a job as quickly as possible. Young children are under their parents' authority just as in the previous example, but the parent's job is to help get them to where they're hearing God and responding to Him as quickly as possible. The child should always value (honor) the parents by coming to them any time there is any question as to what God's will is, but the line of authority should shift to being under God as quickly as we can do it. It is our job to "train up a *child*." We're training them to be self-governing Christians who "know the Shepherd's voice" and willingly follow Him.

> A better way to train children is for parents to work themselves out of a job as quickly as possible.

To continue the driving analogy, we want to make them thoroughly familiar with the rules of the road, and then when they're ready for their learner's permit we let them behind the wheel as long as they're driving responsibly. If they're not driving safely (making bad decisions or acting contrary to Scripture), we take them back and show them where the problems are and how they have "broken" the law, or the courtesies of driving. Then we get them back behind the wheel as soon as the foundational problem is corrected. By the time they're ready for their driver's license, they've had plenty of time behind the wheel. They've been given the opportunity to make mistakes while they're under our supervision so they won't make bigger ones on their own. They've had real-world experience applying what they were taught in an environment where failure is not catastrophic (as with a new spouse and children of their own).

Our family has had the joy of experiencing much fruit in our teens and adult children by rejecting teachings on parental authority, and instead helping our teens learn to hear and obey the Shepherd's voice for themselves. At best, our adult children will give us honor. Honor means "great weight." "Great" does not mean complete and infinite. Only God's counsel demands that kind of obedience. Many well-meaning Christian parents have demanded such adherence, and from what we can see, it is resulting in bad fruit.

Accepting the Unexpected

Unreasonably high standards of courtship are also bearing bad fruit. Parents and daughters in some circles are developing such high expectations that very few young men can attain them. It's true that a young lady should have high expectations for the one to whom she commits herself, but there is a widening chasm developing between reasonable expectations (he loves the Lord, is maturing in Christ and cherishes her above all others), and off-the-chart expectations (he was aware of and followed all the rules of courtship her family had established, received inspection and approval by her parents, step-parents and immediate family members, finished school, begun his career or ministry, doesn't believe in going into debt, has no financial debts or obligations, can fully support her, owns a home, agrees with her parents on or her parent's church on non-foundational points of doctrine, etc.). These types of strong expectations lend themselves to pride and attitudes of superiority. Young ladies can enter marriage with the same high-expectation attitudes they were led to develop in courtship, mistaking high standards for spirituality, thus crushing their husband's hearts.

Marriage takes more preparation of the heart than does singleness. One of the best ways for a daughter to prepare her heart for marriage is to get into the habit of surrendering her expectations to God. She needs to understand that most marriages have their share of unexpected turns, and there is no "ideal" example. A husband's new job may require unexpected travel, or he may experience job changes that require multiple moves or he might be laid off. There may be miscarriages, injuries, illnesses or crises in his extended family or hers that will require at her attention. Perhaps a wife may want to leave work and settle into the making of a home, but her husband decides they need the extra income to get past a financial hurdle, and wants her to continue working for a while.

> Marriage takes more preparation of the heart than does singleness!

In addition, husbands can change. They can fall into sin, or become disabled or die. A wife may find herself in the workforce as Ruth did after her husband's death.[83] We have all heard sad stories of widows who never learned how to balance a checkbook or handle the investments their husbands left behind, and end up making bad decisions. Uneducated, unskilled and emotionally grieving widows make easy targets for scam artists. How blessed a wife will be if she has learned not to be bound to a set of ideals, expectations and rules, but to God Himself to guide her.

Children bring the most obvious changes to a woman's

lifestyle. They come with needs for vast amounts of time, attention, instruction and love. We want to encourage our daughters to consider both the costs and the rewards of motherhood. Jesus gave strong warning about our interactions with children.

> Woe to him who causes one of these little ones to stumble. It would be better for him if a millstone were hung about His neck and he be cast into the bottom of the sea...[84]

If a woman brings children into the world, she'll want to make sure she doesn't live in a way that causes them to continually stumble. That means that a calling a wife may have will need to take a back seat to the time-consuming privilege of training, influencing and loving the dependent and needy future-adults that will be placed in her charge for a very short while.

God used many women in unusual ways down through history. Deborah[85] obeyed God and served as a judge over Israel, leading her nation into victorious battle. She didn't want to do it, and had every reason to decline; instead she *obeyed* the Lord. The daughters of Zelophehad,[86] who didn't allow the rules to keep them from asking the Lord's direction, were the first women to receive an inheritance in their nation.

Daughters don't need to major in homemaking skills to prepare for marriage, either. Those skills can be learned at any time. Our children have all learned pretty quickly about running a home by virtue of living in a family where everyone shares the load. Far more important are the life skills it takes to live in harmony with another person for fifty years or more, not to mention to train children for twenty. There aren't many husbands who would prefer a perfectly organized house, hand-sewn clothes and homemade bread to a spouse with a kind attitude and listening ear. (And the ones who would, we wouldn't encourage our daughter to marry.) A person with a kind and forgiving heart will be much happier in marriage than one who is used to high expectations and having her own needs met.

The most beneficial preparation our children can receive for marriage is the model of a healthy, loving marriage lived before their eyes. How we parents relate to each other and to them *is* the preparation they receive for marriage (whether we realize it or not). And that is a *much* more effective safeguard than the external rules of courtship.

It doesn't take very long, though, for us to realize that we all fall short of being perfect role models for our children. Mistakes, frustration, disappointment, misunderstandings, hurts, learning and growth are the daily realities of where most of us live. It's certainly the environment in which I entered marriage in 1979.

> The most beneficial preparation our children can receive for marriage is the model of a healthy, loving marriage lived before their eyes. That is a much more effective safeguard than the external rules of courtship.

But, a negative environment can turn into great blessing whenever we allow God to intervene. When our children and teens see positive changes where mistakes are being admitted, frustrations handled, disappointments surrendered, forgiveness given and getting up when one falls happening again and again, they take note. And they take heart. They begin to see by example, and not by theoretical instruction, that God is real, powerful, redemptive and loving.

Common courtesies, respect for others and their property, small kindnesses, gentle answers, a sympathetic word and listening ear, along with mutual respect and forgiveness are skills that will serve our children well in singleness or marriage. Some of our daughters will remain single, some will marry, some will get college degrees, some will go straight into careers, some will work part-time and some will be full-time mothers and homemakers. We also know that all of our children will disobey God's voice sometimes – that is the nature of the human race.

> A negative environment can turn into great blessing whenever we allow God to intervene.

Child-bearing

Very devout, Christian people with very different Biblical understandings can, and do, disagree on family planning. It's an issue that should be agreed on between a husband and wife, and based on their own understanding of the Scriptures.

One view is that it is entirely a couple's decision when and how many children they should have. Some couples who adhere to this view practice birth control. Some unknowingly use birth control products that cause abortion. Others use products that don't cause abortion. Some use natural family planning that depends on a wife's natural cycles and timing.

A second view believes that God wants His children to leave the decision to "open or close the womb" completely up to Him. Couples who adhere to this view do not use birth control products or practice birth control methods.

Our children are encountering both of these views as they become adults and begin to prepare for marriage. We'd like to share with you our own understanding of the Scriptures, and what we've discussed with them. We realize that our adult children may come to a different understanding than we have. That's okay. That will be between them, their spouses and the Lord. We believe, however, for our family that we have the mind of the Lord on this topic. We realize, however, that we may be wrong, and we want to stay open to correction, both by the Lord and through our brothers and sisters in Christ.

We first took a look at the view that God wants every couple to leave the decision to open or close the womb completely to Him. We tested it first to see if it held up to the test of the rest of Scripture. What we found were very strong teachings that were based on a just a few Old Testament verses. Of those verses, none were Scriptural *commands* to leave the decision of family-planning to the Lord. On the other hand, we saw an overwhelming amount of instruction to seek the Lord for wisdom and guidance for personal decisions of every sort.

In addition, we saw that God loved to demonstrate His blessing in a physical, outward (visible) way to His children in the Old Testament, but more spiritually and inwardly to His children in the New Testament. Here are a few samplings of His blessings.

Old and New Testament Signs of Blessing

- In the Old Testament, physical children were a sign of God's blessing and a lack of physical children a lack of blessing (Ps 127). In the New Testament spiritual children are a sign of God's blessing, lack of spiritual children a lack of blessing.
- God's command to Adam and Noah was to multiply and fill the earth with physical children. In the New Testament, Jesus' command to His disciples was to go and make disciples (spiritual children) of every nation.
- In the Old Testament physical wealth and riches were a sign of God's blessing. In the New Testament, Jesus teaches that physical wealth and riches are a stumbling block to salvation.

- In the Old Testament houses and lands were a sign of blessing. In the New Testament *giving up* houses and lands (for Jesus' sake) is a blessing.
- In the Old Testament, possessing the land is a blessing; in the New Testament becoming a foreigner and sojourner on the earth is a blessing.

If we were to apply the truth of Psalm 127, for example, that children are a reward from God, to women in this New Testament covenant, what conclusions would we need to draw about women who are obedient to the Lord but cannot have children, or who have multiple miscarriages? Is He not "rewarding" them? Is that how they are to gauge God's rewards to them in this covenant? What about the New Testament promise that His joy is a reward to His children for obedience? It is a very necessary safeguard to weigh everything we hear and read in light of the covenant into which we ourselves are living.

We also took a look at the fruit we were seeing in those who declare that God wants His people to *not* to plan their family size. We see that many mothers don't have the time to give the kind of personal attention young children need to be loved, nurtured and trained. We also see older children and teens overburdened with adult responsibilities and receiving too little nurturing and attention. And a growing number of young people are viewing parenting as hectic, overburdened or joyless. While we have heard the public testimonies of mothers who do not plan their family size say they are fulfilled and joyful, we personally know of very few who have the joy that every Christian knows comes from obeying the Lord. This is damaging to a marriage, to our faith and to our Christian witness.

We do love *children* and have seven of our own. But, we do not love this *doctrine* because we believe it is a swing in reaction to the promiscuous, not-child-loving culture that surrounds us. It has caused its adherents to swing all the way from rebelling against God in their former lives – completely past the central place of hearing and obeying the Lord in their personal lives – all the way over to trying to accomplish God's will in the flesh with rules and laws to guide them. Clinging to a non-Scriptural law rather than seeking the Lord for His direction for our lives robs us of the personal direction and joy that God intends for His people.

We thought, too, about a Christian farmer who might decide to apply this same doctrine to his planting and harvesting concepts. He understands the times and seasons that God created in the world (and patiently waits for the early and latter rains).[87] But instead of planning his crops wisely and in the right season, he decides he can now sow good seed in fertile soil whenever He likes, and trust that God will only let the seeds He wants to grow come up. He wouldn't take into his own hands any scheduling, forethought or planning. He would be free to sow as much seed as he liked without any concern for germination because he now believed that germination was completely in the hands of God. He wouldn't have to plan for resources to tend to a bumper crop because he'd asked God not to allow any of the seeds to sprout that weren't in His will. Such a farmer wouldn't be considered a very responsible steward of any farm God had entrusted to his care.

Jesus forced His disciples to think ahead and think deeply about the sacrifices they'd have to make to follow Him.

For which one of you, when he wants to build a tower, does not first sit down and calculate the cost to see if he has enough to complete it? Otherwise, when he has laid a foundation and is not able to finish, all who observe it begin to ridicule him, saying, 'This man began to build and was not able to finish.' Or what king, when he sets out to meet another king in battle, will not first sit down and consider whether he is strong enough with ten thousand men to encounter the one coming against him with twenty thousand? Or else, while the other is still far away, he sends a delegation and asks for terms of peace.[88]

We believe that God wants us to seek Him for all of our decisions in life, including how many children to have and when to have them. That direction can be very different for each family. When we take the time to seek His face, or sit at His feet as Mary did in Luke 10 (even though she had pressing duties all around), we begin to sort out the issues and gain knowledge about what the Lord really wants us to do. We gain wisdom by asking the Lord for wisdom. And by that wisdom, we can build a house rather than tear it down.

The New Testament doesn't say much about children, but it does speak frankly about marriage. In 1 Corinthians 7 Paul writes to married couples:

- <u>Because of immoralities</u>, each man is to have his own wife, and each woman is to have her own husband. (v.2)
- The husband must fulfill his duty to his wife, and likewise also the wife to her husband. (v.3)
- The wife does not have authority over her own body, but the husband does; and likewise also the husband does not have authority over his own body, but the wife does. (v.4)
- <u>Stop depriving one another</u>, except by agreement for a time, so that you may devote yourselves to prayer, and come together again so that Satan will not tempt you because of your lack of self-control. (v.5)
- It is better to marry than to burn with passion. (v.9)

We saw that Paul didn't instruct Christians to marry "in order to raise up a godly seed" or "to fill the earth." But because of burning passion, because of the temptation to immorality and lack of self-control Paul writes, "Get married! And don't deprive one another!" That sounds like there is supposed to be *much* more to New Testament marriage than simply procreation.

It's also interesting to note that God told new grooms in the Old Testament not to go into the army, but to stay at home for an entire year and "give happiness" to their wives."[89] What a nice thing for God to do. Every good gift comes down from above, and God never, ever changes.[90]

We want to be a people who will listen to the Holy Spirit's direction in our personal lives and obey Him. When we do obey His individual direction to us, He supplies grace and faith. Obedience to His voice is our key to joy, no matter how full our arms are.

When we asked our adult children for their thoughts on this topic, our son, Jon, replied:

"History shows that certain churches fell into error by setting the church itself up above both government and family, investing it with a level of infallibility – those who spoke on behalf of the church could not err because the church was God's authority on earth, and those leaders were under that authority. They also made the church an intermediary between God and man – it spoke for God and listened for God.

Some modern-day teachings on the family appear to be repeating these errors on a different level. Instead of infallible church authority, there is infallible parental authority; instead of an idolatrous focus on a female divinity figure, there is an idolatrous focus on female fertility. Church leaders have been replaced with church

Giving Them the Truth of God's Grace

"patriarchs," the only difference being the level at which they commit the error. One group makes an idol of their church structures; another makes an idol of their family structures."

Here is a testimony from a wise mother who waited on the Lord's direction for a fourth child.

> "My husband and I were both in agreement about the timing of each of our first three children, who were born about two and four years apart. I very much enjoyed being able to spend time with each one, and they enjoyed their time with my husband and me, as well as each other.
>
> When our youngest was about four, I had a strong desire for a fourth baby, but when I discussed the idea with my husband he wasn't in agreement. The Lord had been teaching me about crying out to Him with my desires and not continuing to bring things up to my husband. I began to pray that if having more children was God's plan for our family, that He would change my husband's heart.
>
> One evening during this time, as I was wondering if God would find it His will to bless us with another baby, I heard a whisper in my heart that said, "In My time." How happy I was to know that it truly was God's plan to increase our family!
>
> For the next year I quietly prayed without pressing my husband about the issue. I had learned that the Holy Spirit was the only one capable of changing hearts. One afternoon, my husband came home from work and said that the Lord had changed his heart while he was at the office! It took another

year for us to conceive, but we're overjoyed as we await the arrival of our new gift from the Lord."

> So then we pursue the things which make for peace and the building up of one another...The faith which you have, have as your own conviction before God. Happy is he who does not condemn himself in what he approves.
> ~from ROMANS 14

We would like to add that the children and teens in this family are exceptionally sensitive to the Lord, and have benefited greatly from their mother's one-on-one attention, tenderness, training and love. Her obedience to seek the Lord for timing on receiving children, accept her husband's decision without putting pressure on him, and wait on God's direction for their family is bearing exceptional fruit.

Conclusion

Jesus made it clear that He had little tolerance for people who said they represented His Father, but placed burdens on people that were hard to bear. He warned people to beware of religious leaders who burdened people with loads that were heavy to bear. He didn't say the loads were *impossible* to bear, but that they were *heavy* to bear.

The Apostle Paul also became angry with people who said they spoke for the Lord but tried to place extra rules on the Galatians.

May we teach our children to take the warnings of the Lord Jesus and the Apostle Paul as seriously as they were given, and guard the grace that has been given to them at all cost, never allowing any doctrine of man to encroach upon it.

CHAPTER SEVEN

For Wives Only

Though the influences of television, music and friends described in Chapter Nine of our first book, *Children of Character I*, were first Bill's convictions, there have been many other issues in which I first "saw the light." From financial matters and entertainment, to housing and education, in practical and spiritual matters of every sort, I would often be the first to see the right direction.

Because of my choleric temperament (strong leadership tendencies) [91] and my quick discernment (many of life's decisions appear in the black-and-white of wrong or right), and because of Bill's phlegmatic, laid-back, "always-content" make-up, it seemed natural for me to alert him to all my insights and concerns. It also seemed natural to expect him to respond correctly and quickly. After all, what leader wouldn't want to see a better way? And who wouldn't want to do what was so obviously best for his family?

Much to my amazement in those early days, Bill often wouldn't see or agree. Or he would see and agree, but then not address it. This was both frustrating and confusing for me. *Why would God let me see dangers or pitfalls for us or for our family*, I'd wearily muse, *only to have my warnings fall to the ground?*

It was discouraging. My heart began to grow cold and a bit cynical over many concerns. He and I seemed to be operating on different "pages," and I could tell we were beginning to grow apart. I wanted our marriage to deepen and grow and I wanted our family to grow in love, but I felt that my husband's immobility was holding all of us back from so much good.

One night, as Bill slept soundly beside me, I tossed, silently aching over his unwillingness to follow through on another issue that was important to me, an issue I felt should be important to both of us. As I lay there, listening to his peaceful, unconcerned breathing, my ache turned to anger. As my anger rose, I remembered the last time I was hurt by one of his "non-actions."

Children of Character II

Then I could recall the time before that, and the time before that. I soon had a lamp on, rapidly journaling. Twenty minutes later, my journal had turned into a long list of my husband's sins, which I was surprised that I could recall in such detail. I had told myself it was good to get it all out in private and while I was thinking about them, rather than let those past hurts seep back into conversations later. But my, how that list went on. And on!

When I finished, I read it over again, and was aghast that my husband could rest so blissfully beside me with such a history of past sins! Oh, the pain of not having a real sense of oneness in our marriage, and of not being unified in our goals and desires. And, oh, the ache of feeling like I had to constantly wait for him to catch up or catch on.

Then, in the center of my pain, a clear, logical, sensible thought slipped into my mind.

My, what a fool you were to have married him! If only you had waited, and made a wiser choice, you could have had the husband you deserve.

I had the sense that my hurts had just carried me down some sort of dangerous path, carried me over some sort of line on a road of bitterness I had never crossed before.

This new thought was so logical and so real. It sounded like *truth*. My husband's list of transgressions certainly was truth. But something about this new thought frightened me. It seemed foreign and hollow, as if it were *disguised* as truth, but was really something else. I had the very real sense that my unfulfilled expectations and hurts had just carried me into some kind of dangerous current that was headed toward a huge waterfall. I could tell I was in new unfamiliar waters,

For Wives Only

with a dark, scary foreboding. I somehow realized in that darkness, that it would be darker ahead, and that very bad things that would overpower me if I allowed myself to be carried any further in my bitterness.

Up to that point, the enemy had been my husband's resistance and sometimes even my husband himself as I saw him standing in the way of good. In that moment, my enemy became much bigger than Bill or any of the issues on my list. While I hesitated, something on that dark road of bitterness ahead did its best to beckon me.

Your motives are right! He's just being stubborn. You only want what's best. What could be wrong with that?

Yet, I somehow sensed I was in imminent danger. I knew if I didn't quickly turn back, I might plunge over the falls into a new place of great, cold, bitterness from which it would be very difficult to return.

In the next moment, I climbed out of bed, dropped to my knees and quickly forgave Bill, releasing him from every expectation and hurt on that list. I also asked God to forgive me for not forgiving my husband, and I destroyed the list. I couldn't believe how much lighter, freer, cleaner I felt inside. I felt as though I'd been let out of a prison.[92]

When I glanced over at Bill as I climbed back into bed, I was shocked at how much differently I now saw him. A few moments before I'd been trapped inside a prison of hurts and unfulfilled expectations. The thick bars of my prison had kept me from seeing the *whole truth*. Transgressions were the only truths that had been visible through my bars, giving me a perverted view. I could now see him correctly, as my brother in Christ with strengths and weaknesses, good points and bad, just like me. My skewed perception had been my reality, and now I was free.

That night I experienced an interesting truth, that our view of others (or of ourselves, or even of God) is affected, actually *filtered*, by the state of our own hearts.[93]

> With the kind You show yourself kind. With the blameless You show Yourself blameless. With the pure You show Yourself pure. And with the crooked, You show Yourself twisted.
>
> Psalm 18:25-26

What does that mean? I think it means that many people can look at *God*, who does not change and all see Him differently. Some will see Him as kind, blameless and pure. However, those who are crooked within themselves will only "see" Him as twisted. God will allow Himself to be seen, will even appear Himself as twisted to those who are unable to see Him as kind, blameless or pure. One example of this truth is Revelation 15:6, where those who see with God's perspective are worshiping Him for the very same acts that those with a twisted view are blaspheming Him.[94]

> There is a way which seems right to a man, but at the end of it are the ways of death.
>
> PROVERBS 14:12

In the same way, several people can also look at another *person*, and some will see mostly strengths, while others mostly weaknesses. When my hurt turned to anger and bitterness, a dark filter silently settled over the eyes of my heart, altering my view.

We can also see *ourselves* amiss, either condemning ourselves[95] or thinking too highly of ourselves.[96] It all depends on the filter, the eyes of our hearts. Filters allow certain truths, selective facts, to get into our thinking, while blocking out other facts.

The way that I'd been walking *seemed* right to me. My desires for good, the desires for the best for our family should have been a good path, a safe one. How could it have led to danger? How surprised I was to find my answer in the book of Genesis.

Desiring Good

Genesis doesn't record whether God told Adam that if he ate from the tree of the knowledge of good and evil that he would become wise. Nor does it record the serpent telling Eve that she would gain wisdom. But for some reason, when Eve looked at the tree, she saw something she believed would make her wise.

> When the woman saw that the tree was good for food, that it was pleasant to the eyes, and a tree desirable to make one wise...
> Gen 3:6

Who wouldn't want to be wise, or being wise wouldn't want to become wiser? The Scriptures are filled with commands to get wisdom! What Eve was looking at was so obviously good. Wasn't everything God had made good anyway? It also looked deliciously healthy. Why would God want to withhold something good and healthy? And it was incredibly beautiful (pleasant to the eyes). Good, good, good. And now, the possibility of something even better? Wisdom!

The only thing Eve had to do to get something very good was the obvious –just reach out and take it. I would guess that the longer she looked at it, and the longer she thought about what she might have been missing, the better and more desirable it began to look. And the only small hindrance to getting that good thing was that she'd have to disobey God's one small command – a command she may have heard third-hand through her husband.

Whether Eve was alone when she reached for that beautiful, good fruit or was standing beside her husband, or whether she brought the potential benefits of gaining wisdom to his attention on a date night, or whether she only casually mentioned it because she didn't want to risk being told "no" by an "unenlightened" husband, we don't know. We're not told of how much conversation went on before the first wife fulfilled the first desire for something good, something better, something more. We know that Eve applied some type of pressure to her husband because Adam was reproved by God for heeding the voice of his wife.[97] In the end, Eve decided to make the final decision for herself, and then influenced her husband to join her. She went after something good and beautiful, something that she thought would bring wisdom.

When I place myself in Eve's position, and identify with the pull of her desire for something that she wanted very much that looked very good, I realize that, based on my past behaviors, I probably wouldn't have acted any differently. And when I imagine the sort of reasoning she might have used that would have made it possible for her to justify breaking that one small command, I wince. Had I ever twisted or stretched or openly disobeyed God in order to reach out and grasp for something that looked very, very good?

Surrendering Wrong Desires

When I first came to Jesus, I made many altars on which I'd surrendered *wrong* desires – desires of self-importance, self-centeredness, self-ambition. God replaced those wrong desires with good ones, and I rejoiced.

Surrendering Reasonable Desires

As I grew in Him, I came to a place of dying to certain *reasonable* desires – expectations and conveniences in the midst of raising a large family, such as air-conditioning, nicer clothes and more dependable vehicles. And to the degree that I'd placed those reasonable desires on the altar, they had been replaced by even *better* desires. I began to see the value of my inconveniences in forging new character in me and my children. I saw my children's character was becoming more important to me than any earthly conveniences. New desires for a godly home rather than a nicely furnished one, with wise, strong children, no matter my personal cost, replaced my old reasonable desires.

What joy it was to finally have righteous, good desires. It had been a personal milestone in my Christian life, and it was a satisfying experience.

Surrendering Good Desires

Why then were these new, good desires not being fulfilled? Though I'd traded desires for self-importance in for oneness in marriage, I saw that we were still not one. Though I'd died to desires for reasonable conveniences, and come alive to desires for the best for our family, I felt that the potential fulfillment of those good desires was being thwarted by my husband's non-action. I felt that unless my husband made some changes for us and in our family, that my good desires would never be fulfilled.

> Take My yoke upon you and learn of Me. For My yoke is easy and My burden light.
>
> MATTHEW 11:29

True Wisdom: A Healthy Fear of Disobeying the Lord

How tempting it is for a wife to reach out and grasp for a new truth that is pleasing to the eyes (especially where her family is concerned), that would be good for her family and that would make them all wiser? The only catch is that if we have to violate God's commands to get that which is good, it simply can't bring good.

Once Eve decided to disobey God's one small command, she lost the very thing she was pursuing. She didn't know it, but as long as she was obeying God's one command *(You shall not eat)*, she already had all the wisdom that she needed because "the fear of the Lord is the beginning of wisdom."[98]

Eve lost the very wisdom she had by pursuing *wisdom* more than *obedience*. In the same way, we lose wisdom when we pursue anything more than obedience to God. There's nothing *wrong* with desiring good things for our families or for us. But if we can't live without them, if we have to violate God's commands to reach out and get them, if we believe that we're more spiritual because we see them if our husbands don't, then we, too, become unwise.

When a Husband is Not on the Same Page...

It can be hard for a wife to read a book like this, and then trust God for the outcome of her children when she feels her husband isn't on the same page. Almost every wife I've ever spoken with has felt that way at one time or another to a greater or lesser degree. I certainly have!

Here are a few lessons I've learned over the years that have helped me a great deal. I hope they encourage you.

- A husband is simply a husband, not a savior. True help comes from Jesus Christ.
- A prayer closet can be more effective than a marriage counselor's office.
- The Holy Spirit is a wonderful counselor – whenever I decide to listen.
- A husband doesn't have to be on the same page for God to do a really good work in a family.
- Fathers tend to be firmer, more black-and-white, cut-and-dry, and to the point. That's okay.
- It's better to continue implementing boundaries and consequences a husband has set up if he feels they're best.
- It can hinder progress if we take matters into our own hands to "protect" a child from his father's firmness.[99]

A Note to Dads from Bill

Guys, if you're expecting flowery words and touchy-feely stuff, you're in the wrong place. I've never been accused of pulling any punches or beating around the bush when I speak to fathers. Maybe that's why I've only had two groups ever ask me to speak twice. Amazingly, there are a few men who have actually gone out of their way to listen to me several times at various venues. They probably need professional help.

I'm going to be a little easier on men here than I was in *Children of Character I*. If you made it through chapter Nine of that book without getting mad or walking away bloody (but convicted) it was probably due to Mardy's editing. She's out of town as I finish the final draft of this book, so you're going to get me unedited. You better hang onto this first edition. This chapter may not be here for the second edition.[100]

When I considered marriage I didn't just see "us;" I saw backward. I saw my great-grandparents (one of whom was still alive until well after we married), grandparents, parents, us, then forward to our children and their children and their children's children until we became the great-grandparents. That was one of the things I brought into our marriage: a clear idea of what a family should look like. Mardy had had no exposure to multigenerational families when we married.

The other major thing I came into our marriage with was a lifetime of unconditional love. I knew what it was like to love and be loved. Because of Mardy's background, she had a hard time understanding or accepting unconditional love. I saw generations; she saw a marriage. Even from the beginning, even when things got tough I was always in it for the long run.

It took me quite a while to realize the reason, but when I would say, "I love you," she would often reply, "What do you love about me?" I thought that it was my natural inability to put my thoughts into words that kept me from coming up with good answer. It bothered me that while I knew that I <u>did</u> love her, I wasn't able to put it into words. I tried a few answers, but she always realized that I was only saying those things to make her happy. It wasn't really coming from inside me.

One day the answer came to me: I couldn't put it into words because there was no thing about her that I loved. Don't get me wrong, I didn't say there was *nothing* about her that I loved. There was no thing, nothing that she did or said or anything else about her that I loved. I loved her. I loved the person she was inside, the person that even she didn't know she was. I could see that person and I loved her. Anything I could answer to make her happy was less than what I loved. So much less that it trivialized the love itself if I tried to attach a reason to it.

At first that made her uncomfortable and somewhat angry because it didn't fit her idea of love, an idea that required a tangible reason for love. It wasn't until later that she came to understand that any reason for love could become a reason not to love, if the condition changed. The unconditional love that I had always had for her was the unchangeable. I loved her because of who she was. Since she could not be anyone other than who she was, my love would never change.

As a father, one of the most important lessons you can teach your children is that you love their mother unconditionally. Your love for her, and by extension your marriage and family, can't be dependent on anything that either of you can do. There may be rocky times in your marriage, but the children need to know that no matter what, you love their mother and you love them.

From that foundation, that I love Mardy because of who she is, not because of anything she can do, it's a short walk to explaining to the children about God's unconditional love for us. That He loved us even when we were in rebellion to Him. That once we become His, nothing can separate us from His love. The idea of grace is easy to understand if you already have a foundation of unconditional love. Without it we always have to

To Dads

try to earn God's approval and His love. That breaks His heart.

What follows is a somewhat autobiographical (and I hope somewhat humorous) prayer as a man contemplates what love is. Don't try to read too much into it. I drew on my own experiences to write it, and with the exception of the nineteen year-old, I've applied liberal quantities of literary license. For the original version, see Ephesians 5:25 and 1 Corinthians 13.

Your brother,

Bill

A Variation on a Theme

Hey God, it's me again.

You know, I think I've just figured something out. It does not matter what I say to my wife. It does not matter what language I speak to her in, or what seminars or counseling sessions I attend. It does not matter if I'm the world's best talker. No matter what I do, it is going to sound like a bunch of noise. I'm wasting my breath until I take care of the basics: I have to have love.

It does not matter if I am a modern day Moses and I spend every day face to face with You. It does not matter if I'm on TV seven nights a week telling everyone what You are saying to them right now. It does not matter if I have every degree from every university in the world, or that I have the highest IQ ever measured. It does not matter if I can perform three miracles before breakfast and have a mountain-moving business on the side. If I don't have love, I'm nothing in her eyes. Even if I give away everything I have to try to win her or if I die trying, if I don't have love – I lose it all.

Not that it matters anyway because I'm not the world's greatest talker, or the most spiritual person on the block. I can't remember the last time a mountain paid a bit of attention to anything I said to it. And since I don't really want to lose everything, die trying and still come up as Numero Nada, I think I'd better go work on the fundamentals.

Because I'm <u>not</u> the world's greatest talker or the most spiritual person on the block or the sharpest knife in the drawer and mountains ignore me and lots of other reasons she certainly has every right to be irritated with me. That's not her fault; it's mine. I deserve it. I've got to be patient when I think she should have done something sooner. I've got to be patient when I think she should have waited and now the problem is worse. I've got to be patient when I think we should have left ten minutes ago. I've got to be patient when she needs some time to get over the last bone-headed mistake I made. I've got to be patient when she needs to talk and all I want to do is get some sleep. I've got to be patient when she takes five paragraphs to answer a question that could have been answered either "yes" or "no." I have to be patient always, no matter what. It's my job because love is patient and I'm supposed to love my wife.

I'm going to be quiet and easy to get along with. But I'm <u>not</u> going to be comatose, and I am going to take her out as often as we can, and we're going to have fun. It's going to be the kind of fun she enjoys, not what I like. She does not want to wander around Radio Shack with me and her idea of shopping does not include Home Depot, at least not the hardware aisles. She likes her van and dislikes my truck so we are going to use her car when we go out even though it makes me feel old and wimpy. I'm going to bring her flowers even though I don't understand why she would rather have dead ones than nice potted ones that will keep making flowers forever, but that it just one of the unanswerable questions of the universe, and I'm going to have to take it on faith. I'm going to be kind because love is kind and I'm supposed to love my wife.

I'm not going to be jealous because she gets to stay home with the kids and I have to go to work. I'm not going to be jealous if she does go to work and she makes more than I do. I'm not going to be jealous because she gets asked to speak a lot more often than I do. I'm not going to be jealous because the kids, or the neighbors, or even my own parents like her more than they do me. I'm not going to be jealous because she is a lot smarter than I am in the things that matter. I'm not going to be jealous for any reason because love is not jealous and I'm supposed to love my wife.

I'm not going to brag about what I did at work today or where I went or who I saw. I'm not going to brag about how much I make or how much I gave away or how many little old ladies I helped across the street. I'm not going to brag even if I <u>were</u> the smartest or the best talker or even if I had had lunch

A Variation on a Theme

with You today and You had asked me to move another mountain for You (because I remember from the beginning of this little talk that none of those things impress her). But mostly I'm not going to brag because love does not brag and I'm supposed to love my wife.

I'm not going to talk about people behind their back or make fun of anyone when they're not around. I'm not going to act like I'm better than anyone, especially not my wife, because You and I know me pretty well and we both <u>know</u> that's not true and she has her suspicions; and besides, love is not arrogant and I'm supposed to love my wife.

I'm going to have good manners with people I meet and everywhere I go and I'm going to have especially good manners toward my wife because she is worth it and I'm proud of her and I want everyone to know that I think she deserves the treatment she's getting from me. I'm even going to have good manners when I'm driving and that guy in the red pickup truck just butted in line and made me spill the ice cream I was bringing home to my wife and I'd like to wring his neck and… well, I'm still working on this one, but I'm getting better. I'm going to have good manners because love has good manners and I'm supposed to love my wife.

I'm going to let someone else go first when I know I should be next in line and I'm going to let the kids win once in a while even though I know I can beat them. I'm going to do my job quietly and not make a big deal about what I did so that I'll get a promotion. I'm not going to try for the best seats in the theater or the best table in the restaurant. I'm going to let You take care of that and I'm going to let someone else go first, just please God, don't let it be that guy in the red pickup truck… Ok, I guess I need some work on this one too, but I'm definitely going to let my wife go first because love let's someone else go first and I'm supposed to love my wife.

I'm not going to get angry with my wife or my boss or my kids, even the one that snuck up on me just so see if he could do it while I was praying, and you would think that at nineteen he could find better things to do with his time than to scare his poor, old father who was actually doing something spiritual for a change…well, you get the idea. I'm not going to get angry with my boss even though I know Scott Adams[101] follows him around all day when he needs new ideas. And I'm not going to get angry with anyone who calls me at home on the weekends with ridiculous questions that could have waited until Monday morning anyway. I'm not going to get angry because love does not get angry and I'm supposed to love my wife.

I'm not going to hold a grudge no matter what happens or who does it or even if they never ask forgiveness or even say they're sorry. I'm not going to hold a grudge no matter how right I was and how wrong they were, partly because it's just stupid because it is not bothering them one bit, and if they think of it at all it's just to remember how mad I looked when they did it and I couldn't do a thing about it. But mostly I'm not going to hold a grudge because love does not hold a grudge and I'm supposed to love my wife.

I'm not going to do things that are wrong. I won't participate in them or talk about them or watch them or agree with people who do. I know that means I'm going to spend a lot of time away from a lot of people because most of the rest of the world does what's wrong or at least watches or talks about it or says, "It is none of my business what they do in the privacy of their own whatever." That kind of limits my social life, but that's the way it has to be. And when I <u>do</u> find someone or something that is worthy of praise I'm going to promote it and talk about it and share it with people, even if they make fun of me. Love does not approve what is wrong, but it does rejoice in what is right and I'm supposed to love my wife.

A Variation on a Theme

 I'm going to put up with <u>everything</u> and keep my mouth shut and we both know that putting up with <u>everything</u> is much easier than keeping your mouth shut about it, but unless I want to go back to working on my manners or not bragging I'm going to have to take this one as a package deal or it's not going to work. It's not my job to change anyone else, not even my wife, so I'm just going to have to put up with it. I'm especially going to put up with <u>everything</u> from my wife and always keep my mouth shut even though it really wasn't my fault this time because that is what love does and I'm supposed to love my wife.

 I'm going to think the best about everyone. I'm going to think the best about my wife and my kids, even when they sneak up on me, and my boss, and the people at work and even the guy in the red truck. He probably didn't see me and he might have been taking his grandmother to the hospital, except that there was no one else in the truck and he was going away from the hospital, but he might have been going to pick her up. Yeah, that's it. I'm going to especially think the best of my wife, because love thinks the best of everyone and I'm supposed to love my wife.

 I'm going to hope even when I see other people are letting me down. I'm going to expect the best out my wife and kids and boss and people at work and even the guy in the red truck. They have all let me down, but then again, I've let most of them down too at one time or another. I know they can do better because love hopes all things and I'm supposed to love my wife.

 I'm going to hang on, no matter what. I'm not going to make excuses no matter how tough it gets. I'm going to take whatever flack comes my way in order to make this love thing work. I'm going to take it when I deserve it because I had it coming. I brought it on myself. I'm going to take it when I don't deserve it because I'm sure I got away with a lot more than I should have and anyway, there is no way to get out of it without blowing patience or anger or manners or almost anything else that I've done up to this point. I don't want to go back to the beginning because my wife is worth it and love endures all things and I'm supposed to love my wife.

I'm never going to fail her. At least I'm never going to fail her if there is any way I can prevent it. I know me better than anyone else and I'm sure that I will fail her at some point. But I'm going to try. Sometimes she's just going to have to love <u>me</u> because I'm going to fail. And she is going to be tempted to be angry or hold a grudge or any of the other things we've talked about. And she's going to have a chance to love me so would You help her out with that? But I'm going to try really hard to make sure that she does not get a chance very often because love never fails, even though I sometimes do, and I'm supposed to love my wife.

But you know, even if I do all these things for my wife, but I don't do it for my kids or my boss or the people at work or the guy in the red truck, my wife is not going to feel loved because deep down inside she is going to feel that even though I'm perfect with her, she knows I'm capable of being unloving toward other people and that means that it is only a matter of time before I'm unloving toward her. It's weird, but I see now that I have to love everyone or it won't work for anyone.

Well, thanks for taking the time to listen. You've been a great help.

Amen.

Jesus said, "Follow Me!"

When Dr. Hampton heard that Christian leaders were teaching parents that God wanted them to speak for Him to their older and adult children, he said, "But, Jesus said, 'Follow <u>Me</u>!'" He then shared these passages with us, reminding us that some of the people in them were still teens themselves.

Michael Hampton, ThD
P.O. Box 241
Micanopy, FL 32667-0241

Mt 4:19 And He said to them, "Follow Me, and I will make you fishers of men."

Mt 8:22 But Jesus said to him, "Follow Me; and allow the dead to bury their own dead."

Mt 9:9 And as Jesus passed on from there, He saw a man, called Matthew, sitting in the tax office, and He said to him, "Follow Me!" And he rose, and followed Him.

Mt 16:24 Then Jesus said to His disciples, "If anyone wishes to come after Me, let him deny himself, and take up his cross, and follow Me."

Mt 19:21 Jesus said to him, "If you wish to be complete, go [and] sell your possessions and give to [the] poor, and you shall have treasure in heaven. And come, follow Me."

Mr 1:17 And Jesus said to them, "Follow Me, and I will make you become fishers of men."

Mr 2:14 And as He passed by, He saw Levi the son of Alphaeus sitting in the tax office, and He said to him, "Follow Me!" And he rose and followed Him.

Mr 8:34 And He summoned the multitude with His disciples, and said to them, "If anyone wishes to come after Me, let him deny himself, and take up his cross, and follow Me."

Mr 10:21 And looking at him, Jesus felt a love for him and said to him, "One thing you lack: go and sell all you possess, and give to the poor, and you shall have treasure in heaven. And come, follow Me."

Lu 5:27 And after that He went out and noticed a tax-gatherer named Levi sitting in the tax office, and He said to him, "Follow Me."

Lu 9:23 And He was saying to [them] all, "If anyone wishes to come after Me, let him deny himself, and take up his cross daily, and follow Me."

Lu 9:59 And He said to another, "Follow Me." But he said, "Permit me first to go and bury my father." Jesus said to him, "Let the dead bury their own dead, but you go and proclaim the kingdom of God."

Lu 18:22 And when Jesus heard [this] He said to him, "One thing you still lack: sell all that you possess, and distribute it to the poor, and you shall have treasure in heaven. And come, follow Me."

Joh 1:43 The next day He purposed to go into Galilee and He found Philip. And Jesus said to him, "Follow Me."

Joh 10:27 "My sheep hear My voice, and I know them, and they follow Me."

Joh 12:26 "If anyone serves Me, let him follow Me."

Joh 21:19 And when He had spoken this, He said to him, "Follow Me!"

Joh 21:22 Jesus said to him, "If I want him to remain until I come, what [is that] to you? You follow Me!

OUR ROLE VS. GOD'S ROLE

Our Role as Parents (as Temporary Stewards)	God's Role as Heavenly Father (as Eternal Parent)
Protect them by providing safe environments (as much as we're able) while they're still weak.	**Protect** their souls (as they begin to call on Him) when we can't protect them. **Protect** treasures they lay up in Heaven by knowing and obeying Him.
Provide for them physically (food and clothing, etc.) as well as spiritually (provide a personal witness of God's existence and love).	**Provide** Himself to them for every need, both physical and spiritual, as they begin to call on Him.
Pray for them that they would come to know and love the Lord.	**Draw them** to Himself. **Draw near to them** as they begin to draw near to Him.
Encourage them when they make right choices. (The Apostle Paul praised his spiritual children when they did well.)	**Give them** His joy as they obey Him.
Tell them how much we love them and how much God loves them (very much!) despite their behavior.	**He demonstrated His love for them at Calvary.** *While (they) were yet sinners, Christ died for (them).*
Admonish them when they need it (in a humble way).[102]	**Convict** them of sin.

Children of Character II

Our Role as Parents (as Temporary Stewards)	God's Role as Heavenly Father (as Eternal Parent)
Disciple them by showing them what's right and not just telling them (Let them see us ask forgiveness, rise again after falling, ask God for help when we don't know what to do, stay under authority when we would rather have our own way, obey the Lord even when it hurts, etc.).	**Provide grace** to them when they humble themselves and ask Him to help them change.
Begin to **remove protections** (slowly, carefully) as they demonstrate maturity.	**Provide them with everything they need** to live righteously in this world.
Allow the Lord to become their God, directing and guiding them Himself. [103] [104]	**Become their God**, speaking to them and guiding them Himself. *My sheep hear My voice.*[105]

Acknowledgements

Apart from Me you can do nothing. Jesus

It's with a profound sense of gratefulness that we pen our thanks to the Lord for our second book. Mardy had to do battle with some old foes when we actually sat down to try to get so many of our conversations down on paper – namely "Fear of Man" because we would be letting so many people know our convictions on sensitive topics and "Fear of Doing Something Worthless" because she thought our views might be rejected. But, the Lord encouraged us both, and folks who read the first two editions have encouraged us with their thanks.

I'd also like to take a moment to thank the Lord for Mardy. Homeschooling and writing are really a team effort, but most of the day-in day-out work is all her. Since we homeschool our children she spends a lot more time with them than I get to. Much of what you have read is a direct result of her work and effort. Most of the time I am (and was) involved in setting policy and putting out "fires." I'm a terrible administrator and if it were not for Mardy's amazing gifts in that area we never would have survived. Often I would come up with some crazy idea and she would have to make it work, or convince me that it really was impossible. We have had mostly had the same vision over the years and I've got to give her credit: she usually deferred to my wishes if it came to an impasse. So it is with much gratefulness that I acknowledge her efforts.

We also together want to express our thanks to many others.

~A huge thank you to our children, Jonathan, James, Kate, Daniel, Stephen, Patrick and Joel for letting us once again use your stories to encourage others. And many thanks to the youngest five for pulling together to run the house for five weeks while we finished this manuscript. We're not sure we ever want to see another frozen pizza again but we're so glad you had fun downing all that "bachelor food." Thanks, too, to the oldest five for candidly sharing so many thoughts with us from a teen and young adult's perspective. And for all that editing help, too.

~To Michael Hampton, ThD, and wife, Patty, for the invaluable Scriptural oversight on the manuscript. You can't imagine our appreciation for your sound advice, or our joy in knowing you concurred with so many of our personal insights and lessons. Your love for Jesus is contagious and your ability to see Jesus throughout the Bible inspiring.

~To Pastor Eric Redmond for the numerous Scriptural references (we fondly refer to you as our portable concordance), and all the Scriptural and personal insights. We also thank you for your openness with your life and for your friendship.

~To Nikol Hayden for the hours of work spent cleaning up, editing and formatting the second printing. Your gift of love saved us hours of work, and those little quote boxes really spruced up the pages. Thank you for sharing those talents so freely with us, and for your sweet friendship.

~To Katrine Dunn, Scott and Melinda Griffis, Stephanie Johns, Lori LaBelle, Deb Lewis, Sara Pons and Dee Privette for taking hours out of your packed schedules to proof-read and edit for us.

~To Mardy's "Mom in the Lord" Giny Schlensker for hosting Mardy and the younger children for several days so she could

Acknowledgements

write while the children played (and got spoiled).

~To Kathy Sellers, our children's evaluator since 1989, for being such a "character-first cheerleader" for us, and allowing us to try to pursue godliness for our children before academics.

~To all of the Florida homeschool leaders who have allowed our family the privilege of speaking on character to your groups.

~To Dr. Les and Jolie Emhof for allowing us to share some of the material relating to teens with your community for the first time and on so little notice. Your hospitality is extraordinary.

~To Susan Wright and Verna Groger for teaching Mardy so many practical ways to stay in shape while being cooped up for five weeks with a manuscript! And to Suzanne Farina and Wendy Lilly for the encouragement to stay in good physical shape (even though Mardy sometimes wonders if "desk potato" could be her calling).

~A heart full of thanks to all the moms in Mardy's Moms' Group for your friendships and support, for praying for the manuscript, and for all the notes of encouragement to keep on going. You are much loved!

~Finally, a super grateful thank you to the moms who answered the call for last-minute, crunch-time edits to the 2007 editions of this book: Patti Ballard, Nikol Hayden, Stephanie Johns, Denise Middleton, Carole Palmer, Moira Rusu and Jennifer Walley. Without your help we'd never have made the deadline. We're very grateful!

About the Authors

Bill and Mardy have seven children, born between 1981 and 1995, and have homeschooled since 1986. Together they have written *Children of Character I* and *Children of Character II, from the Early Years to Adulthood.*

Bill served as a Director for the Florida Parent Home Educator Association from 1998 to 2004, and on the FPEA Scholarship Board from 2003 to present. He has worked for Florida Farm Bureau since 1982, now serving as a Senior PC Networking Specialist.

Jon & Sally

Bill and/or Mardy have spoken at numerous parenting, homeschool and leadership workshops in Florida and around the country. Mardy has also written for several national publications and writes an e-mail newsletter entitled, A "Mary" Heart. Mardy currently leads a character-focused Moms' Group in Gainesville, Florida.

A Few More Resources from Bill and Mardy...

Go to www.thefreemans.org/speaking_schedule to order materials or schedule a workshop.

Children of Character I
Children of Character II, from the Early Years to Adulthood

"A 'Mary' Heart" is a free e-mail newsletter written by Mardy to encourage moms to take time each day to sit at Jesus' feet, as Mary did in Luke 10.

Workshops/CDs:
- A Spoonful of Humor
- A Woman's Place is in the Heart
- Children of Character
- Florida Home School Law
- Getting to the Root of the Problem
- Guiding Our Teens to Maturity
- Helping Our Teens to Hear the Shepherd's Voice
- Home and School Organization Workshop
- Homeschooling through High School
- How to Win the Hearts of Your Husband and Children
- How to Do Your Best without Burning Out
- Making Altars, Cutting Ties: Identifying Ties that Bind
- Seven Keys to Winning Our Families' Hearts
- Sharpening Your Student's Skills through Political Volunteering
- Peacemaking Skills for Home and ~~Abroad~~ a Board.
- Protecting the Family
- Teaching Children How to Stand Alone

- Teaching Children to Live for a Purpose Higher than Themselves: The Role of Service in our Children's Lives
- The Differences Between False Guilt, True Guilt and True Conviction
- Traps on the Path to Character: Dealing with Pride, Fear, Guilt, Discouragement and Legalism
- Vignettes of God's Faithfulness: Stories to Encourage and Inspire
- When to Speak, When to Pray

Thank you to everyone who is praying for us, and praying for the families we try to encourage. Your prayers are felt! If the Lord brings us to mind, please take just a moment to ask Him to make His presence known wherever we are speaking and to pour out His grace on families to receive and apply whatever truths He has for each one. Thank you!

Notes

Footnotes

[1] 1 Corinthians 15:33
[2] My brothers, do not all try to be teachers, knowing that we shall be held to a higher standard. James 3:1
[3] Romans 14:23; Romans 5:14
[4] Proverbs 29:25
[5] But if we judged ourselves, we would not come under judgment. 1 Cor 11:31
[6] Matthew 7:17-20
[7] 2 Corinthians 1:6
[8] Luke 16:10
[9] A righteous man falls seven times but rises again.
[10] Many thanks to Nikol Hayden for help in organizing and formatting this chart.
[11] Behold, I stand at the door and knock. If any man hear my voice and open the door, I will come in to him, and will sup with him, and he with me. Revelation 6:20
[12] While we might express our wishes that Uncle Freddy be invited, the final decision remains with the bride and groom.
[13] Matt. 5:43
[14] 1 John 4:19
[15] 1 Thessalonians 2:10-12
[16] This account is detailed in *Children of Character I*
[17] Matthew 10:37
[18] Romans 8:28-29
[19] From *The Seven Habits of Highly Effective People,* Stephen Covey
[20] Job 1:4-5
[21] Matthew 5:23-24
[22] Ephesians 4:31

[23] Hebrews 12:2
[24] Luke 6:45
[25] In 1Samuel 16 Jesse thought so little of David that he had not even planned to present him to the Judge of Israel. After he was anointed, David went back to tending his sheep. Much later, he wrote in Psalm 27:10*
[26] Many thanks to Nikol Hayden for help with this chart.
[27] Not in the sense that our children are swine, but in the sense that pearls of wisdom and truth, though they have great value, are not seen as having any value or use to someone whose has lost interest in receiving our counsel. Matthew 7:1-6
[28] Deuteronomy 5:23-27.
[29] Galatians 3:23-25
[30] 2 Corinthians 3:6
[31] I wrote you in my letter not to associate with immoral people; I did not at all mean with the immoral people of this world, or with the covetous and swindlers, or with idolaters, for then you would have to go out of the world. But actually, I wrote to you not to associate with *any so-called brother* if he is an immoral person, or covetous, or an idolater, or a reviler, or a drunkard, or a swindler - not even to eat with such a one. For what have I to do with judging outsiders? Do you not judge those who are within the church? But those who are outside, God judges. Remove the wicked man *from among yourselves.*
[32] Do not love the world nor the things in the world. If anyone loves the world, the love of the Father is not in him. For all that is in the world, the <u>lust</u> of the flesh and the <u>lust</u> of the eyes and the boastful <u>pride</u> of life, is not from the Father, but is from the world. 1 John 2:15-16
[33] Nevertheless, with most of them God was not well-pleased. For they were laid low in the wilderness. Now these things happened as examples for us... 1 Corinthians 10:5-6

Notes

[34] The idea for this chart came from *The Seven Habits of Highly Effective People,* Stephen Covey

[35] Many thanks to Nikol Hayden for editing and formatting help.

[36] Matthew 23:27

[37] Philippians 2:13

[38] John 3:3; 1Peter 1:23; John 3:16

[39] John 5:39-40

[40] Be diligent to present yourself approved to God as a workman who does not need to be ashamed, accurately handling the word of truth. 2 Timothy 2:15

[41] Brethren, do not be children in your thinking; yet in evil be infants, but in your thinking be mature. 1 Cor 14:20; As for you, the anointing which you received from Him abides in you, and you have no need for anyone to teach you; but as His anointing teaches you about all things, and is true and is not a lie, and just as it has taught you, you abide in Him. 1 John 2:27; For consider your calling, brethren, that there were not many wise according to the flesh, not many mighty, not many noble. But God has chosen the foolish things of the world to shame the wise, and God has chosen the weak things of the world to shame the things which are strong, and the base things of the world and the despised God has chosen, the things that are not, so that He may nullify the things that are so that no man may boast before God. But by His doing you are in Christ Jesus, who became to us wisdom from God, and righteousness and sanctification, and redemption, so that, just as it is written, "Let him who boasts, boast in the Lord." 1 Cor 1:26-31

[42] Acts 17:11

[43] 2 Peter 1:20

[44] 1John 2:20,27

⁴⁵ But the natural man receives not the things of the Spirit of God, for they are foolishness to him. Neither can he know them because they are spiritually discerned. 1 Corinthians 2:14

⁴⁶ Galatians 5

⁴⁷ See to it that no one takes you captive through philosophy and empty deception, according to the tradition of men, according to the elementary principles of the world, rather than according to Christ. Colossians 2:8; These people honor me with their lips, but their hearts are far from me. They worship me in vain. Their teachings are but rules taught by men. Matthew 15:8

⁴⁸ Matthew 15:8

⁴⁹ Acts 17:11

⁵⁰ 2 Corinthians 8:7

⁵¹ 1 Corinthians 9:22

⁵² 1 Timothy 1:9

⁵³ All things are lawful for me, but not all things are profitable. All things are lawful for me, but I will not be mastered by anything. 1 Corinthians 6:12; All things are lawful, but not all things are profitable All things are lawful, but not all things edify. 1 Corinthians 10:23

⁵⁴ Genesis 2:24; Matthew 19:5

⁵⁵ Thanks to Eric Redmond for these thoughts.

⁵⁶ Anyone who loves his father or mother more than Me is not worthy of Me… Matthew 10:34

⁵⁷ Another disciple said to Him, 'Lord, first let me go and bury my father.' But Jesus told him, 'Follow Me, and let the dead bury their own dead.' Matthew 8:21

⁵⁸ Matthew 19:28

⁵⁹ Jesus said, "Come, follow Me!"

⁶⁰ I also put a ring in your nostril, earrings in your ears and a beautiful crown on your head. Ezekiel 16:12

Notes

[61] Nevertheless, with most of them God was not well-pleased, for they were laid low in the wilderness. Now these things happened as <u>examples</u> for us, so that we would not crave evil things as they also craved. Do not be idolaters, as some of them were. As it is written, "The people sat down to eat and drink and stood up to play." Nor let us act immorally, as some of them did, and twenty-three thousand fell in one day. Nor let us try the Lord, as some of them did, and were destroyed by the serpents. Nor grumble, as some of them did, and were destroyed by the destroyer. 1 Corinthians 10:5-10

[62] 2 Timothy 3:14-15
[63] 2 Timothy 3:17
[64] Genesis 24:22-23
[65] 1 Timothy 2:5
[66] 1 Corinthians 7:28
[67] John 10:27
[68] 1 Corinthians 7:37-38
[69] 1 Corinthians 7:25
[70] 1 Corinthians 7:32, 34
[71] Galatians 4:1-2; Ephesians 6:1; Romans 7:2
[72] 1 Corinthians 7:34
[73] 1 Corinthians 7:33
[74] Titus 2:3-5
[75] 1 Timothy 5:14
[76] 1 Timothy 5:13
[77] Luke 2:36-37
[78] Acts 9:39
[79] 1 Peter 3:3
[80] 1 Timothy 2:9
[81] 1 Peter 3:4
[82] 1 Timothy 2:10
[83] Ruth 1:1-5

[84] Mark 9:42
[85] Judges 4
[86] Numbers 27
[87] James 5:7
[88] Luke 14:26-33
[89] Deuteronomy 24:5
[90] James 1:17
[91] For an explanation of temperaments, see *The Spirit-Controlled Temperament*, by Tim LaHaye, or Florence Littauer's *Personality Plus*, Fleming H. Revell, 1992
[92] Matthew 18:21-35
[93] Blessed are the pure in heart, for they shall see God. Matthew 5:8; The commandment of the Lord is pure, enlightening the eyes. Psalm 19:8
[94] Example given by Pastor Eric Redmond
[95] Condemning ourselves is not the same as judging ourselves rightly. Satan condemns. If we judge ourselves, we will not be judged. 1 Corinthians 11:31
[96] Though God calls us "kings and priests," these titles are given as gifts and through no efforts of our own. We are to remain humble.
[97] Genesis 3:17 This does not mean that husbands are never to listen to their wives, only that they should not listen to their wives (or anyone else for that matter) if it goes against God's clear command.
[98] Psalm 111:10; Proverbs 9:10
[99] Unless, of course, it is child abuse.
[100] Wow! It not only made it through several printings of the second edition (mostly because she never read it), it has officially made it into the third edition – and she likes it! She did pull a couple of paragraphs out and put them in our first book. She said they belong there. I think that's a compliment.

Notes

[101] The writer of *Dilbert*
[102] Galatians 6:1
[103] Matthew 28:19-20
[104] Ps 127:3-5
[105] John 10:27